INDIANS OF NORTH AMERICA: CONFLICT AND SURVIVAL

The Indians survived our open intention of wiping them out, and since the tide turned they have even weathered our good intentions toward them, which can be much more deadly.

Frank W. Porter III

John Steinbeck
America and Americans

When Europeans first reached the North American continent, they found hundreds of tribes occupying a vast and rich country. The newcomers quickly recognized the wealth of natural resources. They were not, however, so quick or willing to recognize the spiritual, cultural, and intellectual riches of the people they called Indians.

The Indians of North America examines the problems that develop when people with different cultures come together. For American Indians, the consequences of their interaction with non-Indian people have been both productive and tragic. The Europeans believed they had "discovered" a "New World," but their religious bigotry, cultural bias, and materialistic world view kept them from appreciating and understanding the people who lived in it. All too often they attempted to change the way of life of the indigenous people. The Spanish conquistadors wanted the Indians as a source of labor. The Christian missionaries, many of whom were English, viewed them as potential converts. French traders and trappers used the Indians as a means to obtain pelts. As Francis Parkman, the 19th-century historian, stated, "Spanish civilization crushed the Indian; English civilization scorned and neglected him; French civilization embraced and cherished him."

Nearly 500 years later, many people think of American Indians as curious vestiges of a distant past, waging a futile war to survive in a Space Age society. Even today, our understanding of the history and culture of American Indians is too often derived from unsympathetic, culturally biased, and inaccurate reports. The American Indian, described and portrayed in thousands of movies, television programs, books, articles, and government studies, has either been raised to the status of "noble savage" or disparaged as the "wild Indian" who resisted the westward expansion of the American frontier.

Where in this popular view are the real Indians, the human beings and communities whose ancestors can be traced back to ice-age hunters? Where are the creative and indomitable people whose sophisticated technologies used the natural resources to ensure their survival, whose military skill might even have prevented European settlement of North America if not for devastating epidemics and disruption of the ecology? Where are the men and women who are today diligently struggling to assert their legal rights and express once again the value of their heritage?

The various Indian tribes of North America, like people everywhere, have a history that includes population expansion, adaptation to a range of regional environments, trade across wide networks, internal strife, and warfare. This was the reality. Europeans justified their conquests, however, by creating a mythical image of the New World and its native people. In this myth, the New World was a virgin land, waiting for the Europeans. The arrival of Christopher Columbus ended a timeless primitiveness for the original inhabitants.

Also part of this myth was the debate over the origins of the American Indians. Fantastic and diverse answers were proposed by the early explorers, missionaries, and settlers. Some thought that the Indians were descended from the Ten Lost Tribes of Israel, others that they were descended from inhabitants of the lost continent of Atlantis. One writer suggested that the Indians had reached North America in another Noah's ark.

A later myth, perpetrated by many historians, focused on the relentless persecution during the past five centuries until only a scattering of these "primitive" people remained to be herded onto reservations. This view fails to chronicle the overt and covert ways in which the Indians successfully coped with the intruders.

All of these myths present one-sided interpretations that ignored the complexity of European and American events and policies. All left serious questions unanswered. What were the origins of the American Indians? Where did they come from? How and when did they get to the New World? What was their life—their culture—really like?

In the late 1800s, anthropologists and archaeologists in the Smithsonian Institution's newly created Bureau of American Ethnology in Washington, D.C., began to study scientifically the history and culture of the Indians of North America. They were motivated by an honest belief that the Indians were on the verge of extinction and that along with them would vanish their languages, religious beliefs, technology, myths, and legends. These men and women went out to visit, study, and record data from as many Indian communities as possible before this information was forever lost.

By this time there was a new myth in the American consciousness. American Indians existed as figures in the American past. They had performed a historical

NATIVE
AMERICAN
MEDICINE

NATIVE AMERICAN MEDICINE

Nancy Bonvillain

Frank W. Porter III
General Editor

CHELSEA HOUSE PUBLISHERS

On the cover: A Tlingit shaman's rattle made of wood and inlaid with abalone shells, in the shape of an oyster-catcher bird.

Cover Photo: American Museum of Natural History, photo by Stephen S. Meyers.

Frontispiece: A 19th-century Native American medicine man, photographed by Edward S. Curtis.

Chelsea House Publishers
Art Director Sara Davis
Production Manager Pam Loos
Picture Editor Judy Hasday
Senior Production Editor Lisa Chippendale
Managing Editor Jim Gallagher

Indians of North America
Senior Editor Therese De Angelis

Staff for **NATIVE AMERICAN MEDICINE**
Associate Editor Kristine Brennan
Designer Terry Mallon
Picture Researcher Sandy Jones

First Printing
1 3 5 7 9 8 6 4 2

Library of Congress Cataloging-in-Publication Data

Bonvillain, Nancy.
      Native American medicine / Nancy Bonvillain.
          96 pp.   cm. — (Indians of North America)
      Includes bibliographical references and index.
      Summary: Surveys the Native American healing and health care practices from the time of first European contact up to the present. Includes a chapter profiling some Native American healers.
      ISBN 0-7910-4041-0 (hc).
      ISBN 0-7910-4464-5 (pb)
      1. Indians of North America—Medicine—Juvenile literature. 2. Indians of North America—Rites and ceremonies—Juvenile literature. 3. Indians of North America—Health and hygiene—Juvenile literature. 4. Traditional medicine—United States. 5. Healing—United States. [1. Indians of North America—Medicine. 2. Traditional medicine.] I. Title. II. Series: Indians of North America (Chelsea House Publishers)
E99.M4B66 1997   615.8'82'097—dc21
97-11427   CIP
                                   AC

CONTENTS

INDIANS OF NORTH AMERICA

The Abenaki

The Apache

The Arapaho

The Archaeology
   of North America

The Aztecs

The Blackfeet

The Cahuilla

The Catawbas

The Cherokee

The Cheyenne

The Chickasaw

The Chinook

The Chipewyan

The Choctaw

The Chumash

The Coast Salish Peoples

The Comanche

The Creek

The Crow

The Eskimo (Inuit)

Federal Indian Policy

The Hidatsa

The Hopi

The Huron

The Iroquois

The Kiowa

The Kwakiutl

The Lenape

Literatures of the
   American Indian

The Lumbee

The Maya

The Menominee

The Modoc

The Mohawk

The Montagnais-
   Naskapi (Innu)

The Nanticoke

The Narragansett

Native American
   Medicine

Native American
   Religion

Native Americans
   and Black Americans

Native Americans
   and Christianity

Native Americans
   and the Spanish

The Navajo

The Nez Perce

The Ojibwa

The Osage

The Paiute

The Pawnee

The Pima-Maricopa

The Potawatomi

The Powhatan Tribes

The Pueblo

The Quapaw

The Sac and Fox

The Santee Sioux

The Seminole

The Shawnee

The Shoshone

The Teton Sioux

Urban Indians

The Wampanoag

Women in American
   Indian Society

The Yakima

The Yankton Sioux

The Yuma

The Zuni

CHELSEA HOUSE PUBLISHERS

mission. They had challenged white settlers who trekked across the continent. Once conquered, however, they were supposed to accept graciously the way of life of their conquerors.

The reality again was different. American Indians resisted both actively and passively. They refused to lose their unique identity, to be assimilated into white society. Many whites viewed the Indians not only as members of a conquered nation but also as "inferior" and "unequal." The rights of the Indians could be expanded, contracted, or modified as the conquerors saw fit. In every generation, white society asked itself what to do with the American Indians. Their answers have resulted in the twists and turns of federal Indian policy.

There were two general approaches. One way was to raise the Indians to a "higher level" by "civilizing" them. Zealous missionaries considered it their Christian duty to elevate the Indian through conversion and scanty education. The other approach was to ignore the Indians until they disappeared under pressure from the ever-expanding white society. The myth of the "vanishing Indian" gave stronger support to the latter option, helping to justify the taking of the Indians' land.

Prior to the end of the 18th century, there was no national policy on Indians simply because the American nation had not yet come into existence. American Indians similarly did not possess a political or social unity with which to confront the various Europeans. They were not homogeneous. Rather, they were loosely formed bands and tribes, speaking nearly 300 languages and thousands of dialects. The collective identity felt by Indians today is a result of their common experiences of defeat and/or mistreatment at the hands of whites.

During the colonial period, the British crown did not have a coordinated policy toward the Indians of North America. Specific tribes (most notably the Iroquois and the Cherokee) became political pawns used by both the crown and the individual colonies. The success of the American Revolution brought no immediate change. When the United States acquired new territory from France and Mexico in the early 19th century, the federal government wanted to open this land to settlement by homesteaders. But the Indian tribes that lived on this land signed treaties with European governments assuring their title to the land. Now the United States assumed legal responsibility for honoring these treaties.

At first, President Thomas Jefferson believed that the Louisiana Purchase contained sufficient land for both the Indians and the white population.

Within a generation, though, it became clear that the Indians would not be allowed to remain. In the 1830s the federal government began to coerce the eastern tribes to sign treaties agreeing to relinquish their ancestral land and move west of the Mississippi River. Whenever these negotiations failed, President Andrew Jackson used the military to remove the Indians. The southeastern tribes, promised food and transportation during their removal to the West, were instead forced to walk the "Trail of Tears." More than 4,000 men, women, and children died during this forced march. The "removal policy" was successful in opening the land to homesteaders, but it created enormous hardships for the Indians.

By 1871 most of the tribes in the United States had signed treaties ceding most or all of their ancestral land in exchange for reservations and welfare. The treaty terms were intended to bind both parties for all time. But in the General Allotment Act of 1887, the federal government changed its policy again. Now the goal was to make tribal members into individual landowners and farmers, encouraging their absorption into white society. This policy was advantageous to whites who were eager to acquire Indian land, but it proved disastrous for the Indians. One hundred thirty-eight million acres of reservation land were subdivided into tracts of 160, 80, or as little as 40 acres, and allotted tribe members on an individual basis. Land owned in this way was said to have "trust status" and could not be sold. But the surplus land—all Indian land not allotted to individuals—was opened (for sale) to white settlers. Ultimately, more than 90 million acres of land were taken from the Indians by legal and illegal means.

The resulting loss of land was a catastrophe for the Indians. It was necessary to make it illegal for Indians to sell their land to non-Indians. The Indian Reorganization Act of 1934 officially ended the allotment period. Tribes that voted to accept the provisions of this act were reorganized, and an effort was made to purchase land within preexisting reservations to restore an adequate land base.

Ten years later, in 1944, federal Indian policy again shifted. Now the federal government wanted to get out of the "Indian business." In 1953 an act of Congress named specific tribes whose trust status was to be ended "at the earliest possible time." This new law enabled the United States to end unilaterally, whether the Indians wished it or not, the special status that protected the land in Indian tribal reservations. In the 1950s federal Indian policy was to transfer federal responsibility and jurisdiction to state governments, encourage the physical relocation of Indian peoples from reservations to urban areas, and hasten the termination, or extinction, of tribes.

Between 1954 and 1962 Congress passed specific laws authorizing the termination of more than 100 tribal groups. The stated purpose of the termination policy was to ensure the full and complete integration of Indians into American society. However, there is a less benign way to interpret this legislation. Even as termination was being discussed in Congress, 133 separate bills were introduced to permit the transfer of trust land ownership from Indians to non-Indians.

With the Johnson administration in the 1960s the federal government began to reject termination. In the 1970s yet another Indian policy emerged. Known as "self-determination," it favored keeping the protective role of the federal government while increasing tribal participation in, and control of, important areas of local government. In 1983 President Reagan, in a policy statement on Indian affairs, restated the unique "government is government" relationship of the United States with the Indians. However, federal programs since then have moved toward transferring Indian affairs to individual states, which have long desired to gain control of Indian land and resources.

As long as American Indians retain power, land, and resources that are coveted by the states and the federal government, there will continue to be a "clash of cultures," and the issues will be contested in the courts, Congress, the White House, and even in the international human rights community. To give all Americans a greater comprehension of the issues and conflicts involving American Indians today is a major goal of this series. These issues are not easily understood, nor can these conflicts be readily resolved. The study of North American Indian history and culture is a necessary and important step toward that comprehension. All Americans must learn the history of the relations between the Indians and the federal government, recognize the unique legal status of the Indians, and understand the heritage and cultures of the Indians of North America.

An 1888 photograph of the Tlingit shaman Tek-'ic. Like many Native American tribes throughout North America, the Tlingit of the Northwest regard their healers with a mixture of respect, fear, and reverence.

1

HEALTH
AND ILLNESS

In all cultures, people have theories and beliefs about health and illness. Medical theories often influence how we behave, because all people want to be healthy and live long and happy lives. However, people know that they will sometimes be sick despite all of their efforts to stay healthy. Medical theories attempt to explain how to achieve and maintain health and how to cope with disease and injury. People have ideas about what causes disease and what are the most effective ways to cure it. In all cultures, people rely on their theories of health and illness to give them the best chance of living long and well.

For most traditional Native Americans, good health is thought to be a state of balance and harmony, both within the body and between the body and its surroundings. Healthiness includes the proper functioning of one's physiological systems. It also includes the proper state of one's mind and spirit and the proper relationship with one's social and ecological environment. Native Americans think of health as physical, emotional, and spiritual well-being.

Health is not just something that exists; it is also something that can be achieved. People maintain or recover good health by paying attention to their thoughts and actions as well as by caring for their bodies. One way that a person can stay healthy is to avoid abusing his or her body by exposing it to harmful substances. One must eat healthful foods, drink clean water, exercise and sleep regularly, and avoid excess. Most Native American theories of health stress this moderation in activity and habits. In traditional Native American medicine, it is also necessary to maintain good mental health by thinking positively and to show respect to the creatures and forces of the spirit world through acts of prayer and ritual.

The Mandan shaman Old Bear displays medicine pipes, animal skins, and herbs used in traditional healing ceremonies. One of the most important components in Native American medicine is the patient's belief in the curative powers of the shaman.

Despite these precautions, however, people do fall ill, and all humans wonder why they must suffer. In the 1920s, an Inuit man named Aua took the Danish researcher Knud Rasmussen to the home of his sister Natseq, who was gravely ill. Aua spoke solemnly of his sister's illness:

> Why must people be ill and suffer pain? We are all afraid of illness. Here is this old sister of mine; as far as anyone can see, she has done no evil. She has lived through a long life and given birth to healthy children, and now she must suffer before her days end. Why? Why?

To cope with disease and the death of loved ones, people try to understand the causes of their misfortune. Most Native American theories of illness view disease as a state of imbalance resulting from a physical or mental disturbance of the harmony of the body and its relationship with the natural world. Illness may also result from disharmony with one's family, friends, or community, and it may result from an unbalanced relationship with spirit beings and with other forces of the universe.

Native Americans use a variety of treatments to cure disease and restore health. The first step is to find the reason for a particular illness so that the appropriate treatment can be applied. Some diseases are assumed to have relatively simple causes. Common ailments such as sore throats, earaches, indigestion, and muscle aches and pains are considered temporary and pose little danger to the patient. Patients are instructed to rest and to avoid stress. If treated at all, such minor conditions require simple remedies made of herbs or other natural substances. Most Native Americans have some knowledge of how to use plants and other natural substances to treat these problems. For example, medicinal teas made from roots or tree barks help to

The French explorer Robert Cavelier La Salle claims the Mississippi Valley for France while local Native Americans look on. From the 16th through the 19th centuries, infectious diseases carried by Europeans on exploring expeditions such as La Salle's caused more deaths among Native American populations than did warfare or any other catastrophe.

ease a sore throat or stomach upset, and natural oils applied to rashes or other skin disorders usually provide relief.

On the other hand, knowledge regarding the causes and cures of disease belongs only to a small group of Native Americans. When illnesses involve severe pain or unusual symptoms, or when they do not respond to ordinary remedies, people appeal to healers for help.

Healers are trained to cure illness with natural substances such as plants, tree barks, and animal oils, and they are skilled in massage and bone-setting techniques. More importantly, they are able to perform rituals that will heal the underlying causes of serious or life-threatening disorders. By carefully observing patients' symptoms and discussing their activities, healers determine the method by which they can effect a cure.

Although people everywhere become ill from time to time, the diseases prevalent in different geographic areas and in different time periods vary. By 1492, when Europeans first arrived in North America, native peoples had occupied the continent for about 30,000 years. They had developed economies, family and community systems, and political structures. They had found ways to make use of the natural resources around them, and they lived in relative harmony with their environments. Like all peoples, some became ill from minor ailments such as eye, ear, and throat infections or more serious—and potentially deadly— disorders such as intestinal bacteria, parasites or worms, arthritis, rheumatism, and respiratory ailments. As with all cultures,

Native Americans also suffered and died in accidents, from exposure to extreme climates, and during childbirth.

However, North America was a comparatively healthy place to live during this era. Records and journals kept by Europeans in North America during the 17th and 18th centuries frequently comment on the robust appearance and good health of the natives. One observer of Northeast natives, William Wood, wrote:

> [The natives never experience] those health-wasting diseases which are incident to other countries, as fevers, pleurisies, agues, obstructions, consumptions, convulsions, gouts, pox, measles, or the like; but spin out the thread of their days to a fair length, numbering threescore [60], fourscore [80], some a hundred years.

Similarly, the Baron de Lahontan, while visiting what is now eastern Canada, remarked that the area's natives were "a robust and vigorous sort of People, of a Sanguine Temperament, and an admirable Complexion." In what is now North Carolina, John Lawson noted that aboriginal inhabitants were "never troubled with the Scurvey, Dropsy, Asthma, and Diabetes."

Just as plants and animals are indigenous to certain parts of the world, disease-causing organisms are also indigenous to specific locales. However, North American natives were generally spared the most serious kinds of infectious diseases in two ways: the means by which they arrived on the continent and the manner in which they settled here.

Ancestors of today's Native Americans began migrating into North America approximately 30,000 years ago during one of the ice ages, when extremely cold temperatures turned much of the world's water into vast sheets of ice. They migrated from eastern Asia or Siberia into Alaska across a frozen "bridge" that is know today as the Bering Strait. Because many disease-causing organisms cannot survive in such frigid temperatures, the ice also created a kind of barrier that prevented the spread of bacteria and viruses into the people's new home.

The earliest inhabitants of North America were hunter-gatherers who lived in small groups and constantly moved from place to place for food. Since most infectious epidemic diseases thrive only in large, densely settled populations, these nomadic groups, who left the harmful organisms that grow in garbage and human waste behind when they moved, remained largely disease-free.

A third reason for their good health was the absence of chronic psychological stress. Today, it is generally acknowledged that stress, anxiety, and other emotional disturbances contribute not only to psychological ailments but also to the onset and worsening of physical illnesses. As early as the 17th century, a French traveler named Gabriel Sagard observed of the Huron tribe:

> What . . . helps [natives] much to keep in health is the harmony that prevails among them. They have no law-suits

A 17th-century depiction of a smallpox epidemic among Native Americans in what is now Massachusetts.

and take little pains to acquire the goods of this life, for which we Christians torment ourselves so much, and for our excessive and insatiable greed in acquiring them we are justly and with reason reproved by [the natives'] quiet life and tranquil dispositions.

After Europeans arrived in North America at the end of the 15th century, however, the delicate balance that had existed for thousands of years between Native Americans and their environment was abruptly disturbed. European diseases such as smallpox, measles, and influenza had never existed in North America before that time, and many of the carriers, the people who brought the new diseases, may not have appeared sick and were thus impossible to avoid or isolate.

When a disease-causing organism has existed in a population for many generations, the human body gradually develops an immunity or resistance to it. For this reason, although some people in a community may still become sick when exposed to the organism, most who are exposed will remain healthy. However, when such an organism is introduced into another population whose members have no immunities to it, great numbers of people become sick or die.

Death from European-borne diseases decimated the native populations of North America. From the 16th through the 19th centuries, smallpox, measles, influenza, pneumonia, and other infectious diseases caused more deaths than did warfare or any other

catastrophe visited upon the Native Americans. When Europeans arrived in the New World, more than seven million people already lived there—about five million in the present-day United States and two million in present-day Canada. By the end of the 19th century, Native Americans in what was then the United States numbered about 250,000.

In addition to the obvious human tragedy, the dramatic decline in native populations had social, economic, and political consequences. Entire families—in some cases entire villages and tribes—were wiped out in the span of a few years. The most vulnerable members of these societies, young children and elders, died in great numbers, but scores of men and women in their prime, on whom other group members depended for survival, also succumbed, creating unprecedented economic and social hardships. Because political and military leaders were as likely as others to die from epidemic diseases, community stability itself was also undermined.

Sixteenth-century accounts of epidemics among Native Americans reveal the personal tragedies behind the statistics. For instance, in 1590 Thomas Hariot, a British settler in Virginia, observed that:

> within a few dayes of our departure from everie [native] towne, the people began to die very fast, and many in short space; in small townes about twentie, in some fourtie, in some sixtie, & in one six score [120], which in trueth was very manie in respect of their numbers.

Native American healers employ traditional methods such as steaming, sucking out poisons, and inhaling the smoke of medicinal herbs in an attempt to cure their patients. Because they had no immunities to infectious agents like smallpox, influenza, and measles, the native population in the New World was decimated by these and other European-borne diseases.

Neither the natives nor the European settlers of the time understood how disease is transmitted. Native people interpreted these disasters within the framework of their own beliefs about cause and effect. "They were perswaded," said Hariot, "that it was the worke of our God through our meanes, and that we by him might kil and slai whome wee would without weapons and not come neere them."

In the 17th century, French missionaries living among the Algonkian and Iroquoian tribes of present-day Ontario and Quebec recorded similar Native American interpretations of the devastation that befell them. The Huron population in Ontario, for instance, fell in less than two decades from at least 20,000 at the time of French contact in 1610 to no more than 10,000. Because the outbreaks began only after Jesuits started to live in their communities, the Huron concluded that Jesuit priests had brought the ailments. Because the Huron believed that disease and death were often caused by witchcraft, they

English missionaries among the Massachusetts Indians at Martha's Vineyard. The Wampanoag chief Massasoit lost so many of his people to infectious disease that he gave away tribal land to European settlers, saying, "none [of my people] is left to occupy it."

accused the missionaries of being witches. Most of the Jesuits dismissed the notion, but some perceptive priests did admit the seeming truth of the Huron accusations. In 1640 one priest, Gabriel Lalemant, observed:

> No doubt, they [Hurons] said, it must needs be that we had a secret understanding with the disease (for they believe that it is a demon), since we alone were all full of life and health, although we constantly breathed nothing but a totally infected air.
>
> Wherein truly it must be acknowledged that these poor people are in some sense excusable. For it has happened very often, that where we were most welcome, where we baptized most people, there it was in fact where they died the

most; and, on the contrary, in the cabins to which we were denied entrance, although they were sometimes sick to extremity, at the end of a few days one saw every person prosperously cured.

Algonkians living near the Atlantic coast were among the first to encounter English settlers. In Virginia, the Powhatan chief Wahunsonacock told John Smith, "I have seen two generations of my people die. Not a man of the two generations is alive now but myself." In Massachusetts, Massasoit, a Wampanoag chief, gave away tribal land to English settlers, "for none [of my people] is left to occupy it."

When American settlement expanded westward in the 19th century, the same sequence of European contact and sharp declines in Native American populations occurred. Little Wolf of the Cheyenne noted that many of his people "died of diseases we have no name for." The Lakota chief and religious leader Sitting Bull remarked:

> [White men] promised how we are going to live peacefully on the land we still own and how they are going to show us the new ways of living . . . but all that was realized out of the agreements with the Great Father [the President of the United States] was, we are dying off.

In the early 20th century, Native American populations slowly began increasing, and by mid-century the rate of growth had accelerated. Still, Native Americans make up a small percentage of the total population of both the United States and Canada. While the number of Native Americans in the United States is greater than the number in Canada, the percentage of the total population is higher in Canada; the 1990 United States Census Bureau report recorded 1,959,234 Native Americans in the United States, or approximately 0.7% of the population; a 1992 Canadian census reported 533,461 members of First Nations (as native people are called in Canada), or 1.9% of the country's population.

Although Native Americans today suffer from the same diseases as do other U.S. and Canadian populations, some rates of illness remain higher among Native Americans. Gall bladder disease, diabetes, and tuberculosis, for example, are more prevalent among Native Americans, but they have lower rates of heart disease and of most kinds of cancer. One explanation for the differences is heredity, of course, but lifestyle factors such as exercise and diet probably play a significant part as well.

Today, many Native American communities rely on both traditional and modern medical techniques to maintain good health and cure illness. Although not all Native Americans seek traditional treatments, the medical theories and practices of their ancestors remain an important part of their culture.

A Cheyenne shaman's rattle crafted of rawhide, eagle claws, and horsehair. During Native American healing ceremonies, rattles are often used to call up guardian spirits and to drive out sickness from patients' bodies.

MEDICINES

Traditionally, Native American healers used a wide variety of natural substances to cure ailments. They also used various surgical and physical techniques to heal wounds, extract bullets and other harmful objects, set bones, and relieve localized pain. Certain medical and procedural information was common across all Native American societies, while other knowledge was used only among members of a specific culture or tribe. For example, all indigenous peoples experimented with the medicinal properties of plants native to their area; where similar plants were found in other territories, they became part of a common pharmacology among these groups.

Native Americans believed that the curative power of medicinal plants, herbs, roots, berries, fruit, animal oils, and other natural substances came from both natural and supernatural sources. The power of medicine came from the earth, soil, or animal where it was found, but it also came from the spirit forces that transformed the substance into a healing agent. Healers performed rituals to impart or strengthen the curative powers of medicines. Among the 17th-century Onondaga of present-day New York State, for example, a French priest named Jean du Quen observed:

> [A]ll the village Sorcerers and Jugglers, the Physicians of the Country, assemble, to give strength to their drugs, and by the ceremony performed, to impart to them a virtue entirely distinct from that derived from the soil.

Native American healers were not concerned with how medicines were effective but with the fact that they were effective. Their understanding of the relationship between a specific medicine and improved health was not based on analysis of a medicine's properties but on their observations of its effectiveness. Native American healing and knowledge

This sculpture depicts a Native American treatment for snakebites and other wounds. Using a hollow tube, the healer sucks on the area of the bite to extract the venom before applying roots or herbs to the skin.

of medicine, like Western medicine, were the results of much trial and error. Over many generations, people learned through experience which plants and other agents cured a given ailment. Those substances that most consistently proved effective were eventually used as medicines, and less effective or ineffectual substances were discarded.

Irritations of the skin, eyes, ears, and throat, as well as illnesses affecting internal organs, were treated primarily with medicines derived from plants. Native peoples treated boils and abscesses by applying poultices made of various substances and then lancing boils to draw out the fluid and reduce swelling. Among farming tribes of the eastern United States, poultices were made of heated cornmeal; natives of eastern Canada used warmed or fermenting herbs. Among the Kwakiutl of the Canadian Pacific coast, healers used mixtures of a slimy fungus called "rotten on the ground" to cure skin problems. A similar treatment was used by 17th-century Native Americans living in the present-day Carolinas; they used the "rotten grains of Indian Corn, beaten to a Powder and the soft Down growing on a Turkey's Rump."

Burns and scalds were treated by similar methods. Native Americans in the Northeast used a tobacco solution to "wash the sore therewith, and strew on the powder of dried tobacco." Some southeastern tribes preferred an ointment made of tulip tree buds; people in the eastern and central woodlands treated burns with the boiled bark of elm, pine, and basswood trees. The Dakota, Pawnee, and other central Plains groups treated burns with cattail down, which they also used as a powder to prevent their infants' skin from chafing. The Kwakiutl prepared burn remedies from sea animals and plants, including skate liver, seal blubber, and kelp leaves.

To protect skin from sun, wind, and extreme heat and cold, most native peoples generally applied ointments made from either plants or animal grease. Bear grease in particular was a popular salve in the North, East, and West. Northeastern tribes favored protective ointments such as fish oil and eagle and raccoon fat.

Native American healers were apparently expert at treating snakebites and other wounds. For bites from poisonous snakes, they would suck on the area of the bite to draw out the venom and then apply roots or herbs to the skin. Victims of snakebites also ate medicinal roots or drank them in teas. John Lawson's 1714 history of North Carolina noted that the "Indians are the best Physicians for the Bite of these and all other venomous Creatures of this Country. There are four sorts of Snake-Roots already discovered, which Knowledge came from the Indians, who have performed several great Cures."

Native American skill in treating wounds and preventing excessive bleeding was also highly regarded by European observers. One early 19th-century historian maintained, "I have known them [Native American healers] to stop hemorrhagies which I am persuaded would otherwise have proved fatal." Various substances derived from plants and animals were used to stop bleeding. Spiderwebs were applied to wounds by the Mohegan of the East, the Apache of the Southwest, and the Kwakiutl. Others applied mixtures of pounded leaves and berries. Some groups throughout North America found that spores or heads of puffballs (prairie mushrooms) were effective. Among the Dakota of the Plains, these were also applied to the umbilici of newborn infants.

Native Americans were highly successful at treating wounds caused by arrows or bullets. Most effective were various oils and resins derived from trees, especially elm. A 17th-century New England settler observed:

> Some of them have been shot in at the mouth, and out of the ear, some shot in the breast; some run through the flank with darts, and other desperate wounds, which either by their rare skill in the use of vegetatives, or diabolical charms, they cure in a short time.

For internal ailments such as indigestion, bowel disturbances, and dysentery, teas made from boiling roots, leaves, or herbs were used. Plains and western Native Americans such as the Cheyenne drank boiled sweet flag or calamus, a marsh herb, while Utes relied on boiled sand puff. For serious and painful cases of indigestion, the Papagos of Arizona drank a tea made of red earth and boiled water, to which they added a small amount of salt. The Illinois and Miami of the Midwest ingested small pellets of green earth or clay for similar problems.

Bouts of dysentery from contaminated drinking water were also treated with herbal teas. The Huron drank the juice of cedar leaves and branches; similarly, the Onondaga concocted blackberry-root tea and the Delaware used Indian turnip or a woodland herb known as jack-in-the-pulpit. Emetics, which induce vomiting, were frequently administered before the primary treatment to clear the stomach. People suffering from dysentery or other digestive complaints were also put on a restricted diet of bland gruel or broth.

Pinkroot, a plant related to the poisonous nux vomica, was used to treat intestinal worms in the Southeast, as were wormseed and Jerusalem oak. In the Northeast and the Midwest, boiled roots of wild plum, wild cherry, or horsemint were administered. For constipation, remedies called cathartics, or laxative agents, were ingested (the boiled bark of slippery elm, for example). The Dakota, Ponca, and Winnebago treated more serious cases with a solution of water and a root bark called koch, which was injected into the patient's rectum with a syringe made of hollow bone and animal bladder.

Muscle and joint complaints caused by extreme temperatures or wet weather, such as rheumatism, arthritis, and joint swelling, were alleviated by applying salves made from animal fat or by steaming the affected area with burning dried flowers and hair. For respiratory ailments brought on by the same climate conditions, the Winnebago, Dakota, and other Plains tribes made teas from skunk cabbage. The Rappahannock of the Southeast drank a mixture of red cedar berries and wild ginger to aid their recovery.

Another Native American treatment for respiratory problems such as pleurisy was described by the 19th-century observer John Hunter:

> [Natives would] fill skins with hot ashes and apply them over the pained parts, and sweat most violently. Whenever the patient begins to sweat freely, the hard breathing and pain abate, and when the discharge of mucus from the mouth commences, they say [the patient] is out of danger.

For bone, muscle, and joint injuries, Native Americans devised splints from soft wood such as cedar, padded with clay or animal hide for a close fit with the injured part. Patients with soft-tissue injuries were treated with pain-relieving medicines and ointments and received massages to relax and strengthen damaged areas.

Toothaches were treated by having the patient chew a piece of prickly ash tree, dogwood, or buttonbush bark, or leaves of sweet bay (also known as laurel), found along the Atlantic coast and in the South. In some cases, a small piece of wet tobacco was placed in the cavity of a decaying or painful tooth. When all else failed, the tooth was extracted by punching or hitting it with a stick.

A Shawnee medicine man performs a ritual chant while preparing a curative mixture. Displayed nearby are healing ingredients such as animal skin, feathers, and bones, as well as a medicine bag and pipe.

Patients suffering from fevers of unknown origin generally were treated with medicinal agents that induced sweating or by being confined in specially constructed sweat lodges. Most common among the plant remedies for reducing fever were teas made from the bark of several trees, including dogwood, yellow poplar, and wild cherry. Various roots and leaves were also used to reduce fevers.

Indeed, sweat therapy was an all-purpose remedy for many tribes and was usually used in conjunction with other treatments of physical, psychological, or spiritual ailments. An 18th-century French observer described an Iroquois sweat bath as follows:

The sweat bath is a little round cabin 6 or 7 feet high with room for seven or eight persons. This cabin is covered with mats and furs to protect it from the

Among the many botanical agents used by Native Americans to cure disease are the jimson weed (left) and the witch hazel plant (right). Jimson seeds were used to produce visions and were a primary ingredient in poultices applied to burns and inflammations. A distilled solution containing the bark and twigs of witch hazel, commonly used today as an astringent, was used by Native Americans to stop bleeding.

outside air. In the middle of it they put, on the ground, a certain number of cobbles, which they have left for a long time in the fire until they have been thoroughly heated, and above these they suspend a kettle full of cool water. Those who are to sweat themselves enter this cabin nude, and having taken their places, they begin to stir extraordinarily, and to chant, each his song.

From time to time, when the stones begin to lose their action, they revive them by dousing them with a little of this cold water which is in the kettle. This water no sooner touches the stones then a vapor arises which fills the cabin and greatly increases the heat in it. They throw in each others' faces this cool water in order to prevent themselves from fainting away.

Native Americans generally believed that cleanliness in one's surroundings and in one's body was essential for good health. Those who lived near rivers and lakes bathed frequently, even in cold weather. Plains and Southwest natives cleaned their hair with soap made from the roots of yucca plants, and some used tree-bark resin or white clay to keep their teeth clean.

Native American childbirthing methods relied heavily on paying close attention to the mother's body. Unlike European and modern American methods of childbearing, in which the mother gives birth lying down, Native Americans squatted, knelt, or crouched on hands and knees, sometimes holding onto or pulling against a rope or stick. These positions relied on gravity to ease the process. During labor, female attendants massaged the mother's abdomen to help expel the child.

More complicated births, involving long or hard labor, were treated with medicine and additional massage techniques. Native American mothers in North Carolina sometimes ingested a powder made from rattlesnake tails; others drank teas of poplar, wild cherry, or dogwood tree bark, or a mixture of sumac leaves and berries. Zuni mothers in the Southwest ingested a fungus called corn smut to shorten difficult labors.

Although we tend to think of contraception as a modern idea, native peoples relied on a range of vegetable substances to prevent conception. Some were thought to result in sterility; others had only temporary effects. Teas made from roots of dogbane (a chiefly tropical plant), Indian turnip, wild ginger, milkweed, antelope sage, stoneseed, and rosemary were consumed by women and in some cases—as with the Navajo—by men as well.

As doctors of all cultures do, Native American healers relied on two other means of cure: time and the patient's belief in the healer and his methods.

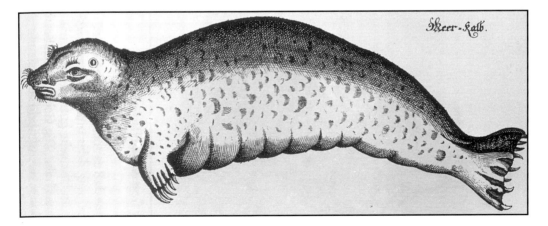

The fat of sea animals such as this seal was used by Native Americans in burn remedies, in ointments for chafed or sunburned skin, and for the treatment of muscle and joint inflammation.

A sweat lodge in South Dakota with its covering partly raised. In the foreground are rocks that will be heated, taken into the lodge, and sprinkled with water to produce steam. During sweat therapy, the animal skin is pulled down to cover the twig frame completely.

Many ailments that are not life-threatening and do not have long-term debilitating effects can be relieved without medical treatment simply by the passage of time. However, when patients receive medicine for a disease, they usually attribute recovery to the effectiveness of the medicine, even when that substance may have no curative properties. Because Native American healers and their patients shared the same beliefs in the healing powers of the substances that were prescribed, and because they shared beliefs about the supernatural powers of medicine, these substances were believed more effective in curing ailments. The patient's faith in the healer's methods was one of the most important components of the healing process.

After the arrival of Europeans in North America, the introduction of infectious diseases previously unknown to natives caused new problems for their medical systems. Most potentially deadly European diseases could not be cured with traditional remedies (in fact, illnesses like smallpox and measles were not curable by European doctors either). However, some noninfectious conditions did respond to newly devised native therapies. Natives of British Columbia successfully treated diabetes, for example, with tea made from the root bark of a prickly shrub called devil's club. Cases of gout, which increased after rum and other alcoholic beverages were introduced to Native Americans, were relieved with an application of medicinal roots and red wine.

Venereal (or sexually transmitted) diseases such as syphilis and gonorrhea were brought to North America by Europeans as well (although syphilis probably originated in Central or South America). Native American remedies included roots of prickly ash, thistle, wintergreen, and wild indigo. Even cholera, a contagious bacterial disease marked by severe intestinal distress, was apparently relieved by a common Native American remedy, according to historian Melvin Gilmore:

> In the year 1849-1850, Asiatic cholera was epidemic among the Teton Dakota. Many of the people died and others scattered in panic. Red Cloud [a noted Oglala healer and civil leader] tried various treatments, finally a decoction [concentrate] of cedar leaves. This was drunk and was used also for bathing, and is said to have proved a cure.

Because Native Americans traditionally have believed that patients cannot be cured unless they have faith in the healer who treats them, the right to call oneself a healer comes after a long and difficult training process—and involves contact with supernatural beings with the power to heal and to punish.

An Assiniboin man holds a slain eagle. Many Plains Indians believe that the spirits of eagles and other animals possess great healing powers.

HEALERS

As is true in nearly all societies, Native Americans first tried to cure themselves of illness with commonly known remedies or procedures: they rested, modified their diets, took curatives, and relied on family members for assistance. When an illness or injury did not respond to simple treatment or when it worsened, however, Native Americans consulted specialized healers whose medical knowledge and expertise exceeded their own. Traditional healers, who still practice today, are trained in diagnostic and medical skills. They observe patients' symptoms and use ritual means to gain knowledge of the impact of the spirit realm on human health.

Healers acquire their powers through various means. First, they must learn to recognize medicinal plants and other curative substances found in their environment and determine the proper dosages of these cures for each condition. They are trained in massage, object extraction, and other manipulative methods used to heal wounds, sprains, broken bones, and other injuries. Their final task—the most difficult and dangerous—is to acquire the means to receive supernatural guidance, because the power of medicine is believed to flow directly from the spirit realm. When the healer is in contact with spirit beings, he or she is at the mercy of unpredictable and uncontrollable forces.

Aspiring healers usually learn practical skills by becoming apprentices to already established doctors. The novice accompanies the doctor in collecting medicinal substances and then observes and assists in treatments. However, prospective healers must use other means to acquire the spirit knowledge necessary to effect cures. Some actively seek supernatural knowledge by praying or questing for visions; others receive powers spontaneously in dreams or in visions.

A Menominee medicine woman, 1916.

Isaac Tens, a Gitskan healer in British Columbia, recounts his experience with the supernatural that led him to become a doctor:

When I was thirty years old, I went up into the hills to get firewood. While I was cutting up the wood, it drew dark towards the evening. Then a loud noise broke out over me, and a large owl appeared to me. The owl took a hold of me, caught my face, and tried to lift me up. I lost consciousness. As soon as I came back to my senses I realized that I had fallen into the snow.

I stood up and went down the trail, walking very fast. On my way, the trees seemed to shake and to lean over me; tall trees were crawling after me, as if they had been snakes. When I got home, I fell into a sort of trance. Two healers came and tried to bring me back to health. When I woke up and opened my eyes, I thought that flies covered my face completely. I looked down, and instead of being on firm ground, I felt that I was drifting in a huge whirlpool. One of the healers told me that the time had arrived for me to become a healer like him. But I did not agree; so I took no notice of the advice.

Another time, I went to my hunting grounds on the other side of the river. After awhile, as I glanced upwards, I saw an owl at the top of a high cedar. I shot it, and it fell down in the bushes close to me. When I went to pick it up, it had disappeared. When I was walking back, I heard the noise of a crowd of people behind me. The voices followed in my tracks and came very close. Then I wheeled round and looked back. There was no one in sight, only trees. A trance came over me once more, and I fell down, unconscious. Later, when I got home, my heart started to beat fast, my flesh seemed to be boiling, my body was quivering. While I remained in this state, I began to sing. A chant was coming out of me without my being able to do anything to stop it. Many things appeared to me: huge birds and other animals. They were calling me. Such visions occur when a man is about to become a healer; they occur of their own accord. The songs forced themselves out complete without any attempt to compose them.

Sanapia, a contemporary Comanche healer, was trained in doctoring skills by her mother and her mother's brother. Both were "Eagle Doctors," whose curing powers derived from eagle spirits. Among the Comanche, healers usually select their successors from among close kin, preferably passing medical knowledge from mother to daughter. Although Sanapia was trained by her relatives, her healing powers come from supernatural helpers, who appear in dreams and visions and teach her songs and prayers to use when she cures. Sanapia credits the eagle spirits as the source of her healing power:

> The eagle got more power than anything living. It's got medicine to help people get well, to cure them. I got power like that eagle cause the eagle helped me and I call on it when I doctor. My mother told me that I'd be just like that eagle when I doctor. I can feel the eagle working in me when I doctor and try hard to get somebody well.
>
> When my mother gave me that eagle song she told me, "When you don't have no place to go for help, when you got no one to lean on for help, sing this song. What you want, you're gonna get. I'll be listening to you. When you sing this song, I'm gonna hear you singing and I'm gonna help you."

In some cases, those interested in learning doctoring skills ask an established healer to teach them. They may also seek supernatural aid directly through fasting, prayer, and offerings. Crashing Thunder, a Winnebago man, relates that he was advised by his healer father:

> You are to fast. If you are blessed by the spirit and breathe upon people you will bring them back to life. If you will be able to do this [cure the sick] you will be of even more than ordinary help to your fellow men. If you can draw out pain from inside the body you will be of aid to all your fellow men and they will greatly respect [you]. After your death people will speak about your deeds forever. In life they will say "really, he has power."

Crashing Thunder was instructed in the proper handling of medicines:

> If you make proper offerings to your medicine, and if you speak of your medicine in the way you are accustomed to do, and if then you ask your medicine to put forth its strength in your patient's behalf, the medicine will do it for you. If you make good offerings of tobacco to your plants, if you give many feasts in their honor, and if you then ask your medicine to put forth their strength, and if you talk to them like human beings, then most certainly will these plants do for you what you ask. Medicines are good for all purposes[;] that is why they were given to us. We are to use them to cure ourselves of sickness. Earth-maker gave them to us for that purpose.

After one receives a calling or has contact with the spirit world, formal training may begin. During a lengthy apprenticeship, an aspiring healer learns how to use natural remedies, acquires the skills needed to perform manipulative and surgical techniques, and achieves the power to draw on supernatural forces to diagnose and cure ailments. The Gitskan healer Isaac Tens went into a full year of seclusion in his father's house, attended only by four male relatives who were also established healers. In addition to songs and chants used in Gitskan curing, Tens also learned how to dream and to enter an altered state of consciousness called a trance to acquire his own songs. "I had to have dreams before being able to act," he explained. When his seclusion ended, his teachers performed a strengthening ceremony that marked his beginning as a healer. "We look at the patient and diagnose their ailment," his teachers told him. "Sometimes it is a bad song within him or her, sometimes a narhnorh [a spirit]." Tens began curing in a "probationary" period, during which he was required to consult with his mentors.

For the Comanche healer Sanapia, who began the process when she was a girl, similar training lasted four years. During that time, she learned doctoring techniques in two stages. First, she acquired practical skills, such as identifying and collecting medicinal plants and learning how to administer them. She also learned the prayers and rituals that accompany the proper collection of medicines.

In the second phase of training, Sanapia functioned as an apprentice to her mother and her mother's brother. She learned how to diagnose and cure illnesses and how to gain access to the eagle spirits who would help her cure. Healing power, she was told, came not from herself but from the spirits.

When her teachers thought that she was ready to begin healing on her own, Sanapia participated in special ceremonies marking the end of her training. Her mother, maternal uncle, maternal grandmother, and paternal grandfather all conferred approval in separate blessing rites. Sanapia's mother ended the ceremonies by giving power to Sanapia's mouth and hands, believed especially important since healing powers come from the spirit world through them and then exit from them when the healer treats patients. The transmission ritual required that hot coals be placed in Sanapia's hands, but instead of feeling heat and pain, Sanapia felt something that astonished her:

> I was sure scared then, almost got up and ran away. I was only a young girl at that time, but, when I took them coals on my hand, inside and outside my hand I felt a chill. Oh, it was like chills in my hands. That has the meaning that power was in there, working in my hands. Felt like it would go up my arm even.

Both Isaac Tens and Sanapia describe the fear they experienced during their initiation and training. When performing cures, the healer is believed to be in the presence of dangerous and powerful spirits and becomes aware that, although one can draw on such power, it cannot be controlled completely. In the words of Black Elk, a 19th-century Oglala Lakota healer and visionary, "If I thought that I was doing it [performing cures] myself, the hole would close up and no power could come through."

While in training and throughout their practices, healers collect plants and other remedies and keep a supply on hand to treat common complaints. In addition, objects of spiritual significance, such as animal teeth and bones, eagle and owl feathers, small stones, and other seemingly ordinary items, are collected during visions and dreams and are thought to be tokens from the supernatural realm that become endowed with special healing properties.

Both types of medicine are stored in medicine bags—traditionally fashioned from soft animal hides, although today the bags are often made of other material, such as a scarf or blanket. Each kit is different, but the contents of Sanapia's medicine bag are typical of the kinds of remedies healers carry: red cedar, juniper, mescal bean, rye grass, prickly ash, iris, sweet sage, milkweed, and peyote, and non-botanical medicines such as crow feathers, glass slivers for making incisions, a sucking horn to extract foreign objects, charcoal, white otter fur, porcupine quills, animal bone fragments, and a tail feather from a golden eagle.

Native American healers are expected to possess not only the knowledge and skills to cure illness but also the personality traits most admired in their communities: modesty, generosity, kindness, tolerance, and evenness of temper. In most Native American communities, healers serve all who consult them. It is considered inappropriate—and possibly dangerous—for a healer to refuse to treat a patient. After all, spirits give the curing powers and intend that they be

An Apache medicine man named Jim. The painted hide to his left was probably worn during healing ceremonies.

used. A healer's refusal to perform a cure could be interpreted as a display of arrogance. In some societies, a refusal meets with a more sinister interpretation. According to Isaac Tens:

> Should a healer refuse to doctor a patient, [the healer] might be suspected of being himself the cause of the sickness, or of the death should it occur. In this eventuality, the relatives [of the deceased] would seek revenge and kill the one suspected. This was the hard law of the country. But the doctors were not known to decline any invitation to serve the people in need.

A Menominee medicine bag fashioned from beaver skin. Though healers collect objects of personal significance, their medicine bags usually contain standard botanical healing agents and instruments.

While healers rarely, if ever, refuse a request for aid, neither do they approach an individual who needs treatment; rather, the patient or a family member comes to the healer. To suggest that one can cure a patient before being asked might be interpreted as a sign of boasting and self-importance and could arouse the anger of the spirits on whom the healer's skills depend. This could lead to sickness or death for the healer.

Native American doctors are paid for their services. Payment for such service varies depending on the seriousness of the ailment and on the ability of the patient and family to pay. Cures for grave illnesses, which require healers to put themselves at risk, are more costly than cures for minor or common ailments. However, if a patient has few means, a token gift is sufficient, no matter how dangerous the curative process may be to the healer.

In traditional communities, healers are highly respected, not only because they do good for people, but also because they are thought to have access to spirit powers far greater than that of ordinary individuals. In some communities, however, the respect given to healers is tinged with suspicion; since healers have knowledge of the causes of illness, it is believed that they can use this knowledge to harm as well as to cure. One example is the Gitskan, who believe that doctors who refuse to cure a particular patient might themselves have caused the illness. Among the Inuit of the Canadian and American Arctic, this attitude is especially strong;

An Apache shaman and his family at home, where an individual who needs treatment would visit him. A healer who approaches a patient before being asked is often considered boastful and could arouse the anger of the spirit powers.

in fact, healers are commonly suspected to be witches. Among the Navajo of the Southwest, healers administer medicines to their patients only after they have tasted a small bit of the medicine themselves to prove publicly that the medicine is not harmful.

Though highly regarded in their communities, Native American healers are required to follow specific restrictions on their behavior. These restrictions, called taboos, include prohibitions on eating certain foods or engaging in otherwise normal behavior. The Comanche healer Sanapia, for example, is not permitted to eat eggs or the internal organs of animals. Kwakiutl healers are not permitted to laugh, sing love songs, or wail after the death of a relative (a traditional act of mourning). Upon beginning their healing careers, Kwakiutl are also forbidden to engage in sexual activity for a time ranging from several months to four years. Isaac Tens reflects on the difficulties of being a healer: "All the medicine men eventually die a very hard death," he says, "because they are not truly human."

The healer's ceremonial treatment of illness involves musical instruments such as rattles and drums, complex songs and song cycles, and movement or dance. While some treatment processes are brief, others are lengthy and complex. Navajo healers, for instance, are skilled in the long and elaborate rituals that cure patients of contaminating entities. The rituals, called chantways or sings, are of many types, depending upon the specific cause of the patient's illness. In general, sings produce cures by attracting the spiritual powers of the Holy People, the deities of the Navajos. Curing sings last two, five, or nine nights, a night being counted from sunset until the following sunset. Each sing consists of separate rites that must be performed in a specific order. Sings often begin with a cleansing bath for the patient, followed by prayers and chants to attract Holy People and motivate them to use their great powers to remove the harmful effects of the contaminating agents.

Navajo healers also possess ritual paraphernalia that have healing powers, including feather wands, painted prayer sticks, small pieces of turquoise and crystal, cornmeal, corn pollen, and herbal medicines. Healers touch these powerful objects to a patient's body, transferring the curative forces of the object to the patient. In addition, Navajo healers attract and transfer beneficial supernatural powers by using dry paintings, which are images made with sand colored with different pigments. Healers sprinkle the colored sand on the ground in complex designs to produce stylized images of Holy People. Most dry paintings are about 6 feet in diameter, although some are as large as 20 feet across. When the dry painting is completed, the patient sits on a portion of the painting. The healer moistens his or her palm with medicinal water and touches the painting so that the colored sand adheres to the healer's hand. The healer then applies the sand to the patient's body and repeats this process, using sand from different portions of the painting and applying it to comparable parts of the patient's body.

The dry painting rite illustrates the Navajo's philosophical emphasis on the wholeness of the body. A patient's pain may appear to be localized, but since the disharmony of body and mind is thought to cause disease, the patient's whole body is treated. Since the external environment also has an effect on human health, natural forces must be kept in balance as well. The following excerpt from a long healing prayer

continued on page 49

INSTRUMENTS OF HEALING

The soul catcher was one of the most important instruments in Native American medicine. This Tlingit version is made of animal bone and abalone shell.

During healing ceremonies, shamans often wore masks, such as this 19th-century Native Canadian mask of wood and abalone. Each one was fashioned to represent the appearance or characteristic of an appropriate spirit power.

The spirit of death is represented by the inverted eyes of this shaman's mask from the Northwest coast.

A beaded Ojibwa medicine bag. By the mid-19th century, such bags were larger, primarily made of trade cloth, and more heavily beaded than were 18th-century bags.

This Ojibwa medicine bag from the Minnesota White Earth Reservation is made of cloth decorated in a beaded floral design.

The medicine bundle shown here belonged to a member of the Weasel Chapter of the Crow Tobacco society. The distinctive design of the bag distinguished the chapter members from other society divisions. During ceremonies, the bundle was opened and women danced with the weasel skins to obtain supernatural power, as promised by the Weasels in a vision, that would ensure the fertility both of the sacred tobacco plant and the Crow tribe itself.

The buffalo horns attached to this headdress, which was worn by a member of the Buffalo Horn Society of the Blackfeet, signify that the owner possessed the animal's fortitude and strength. Blackfeet doctors also treated the tribe's animals and gave charms to warriors to ensure their success in battle.

This fan, fashioned from an eagle wing, was part of the paraphernalia of a Crow shaman. It was used during rituals to call on the sacred power of the eagle.

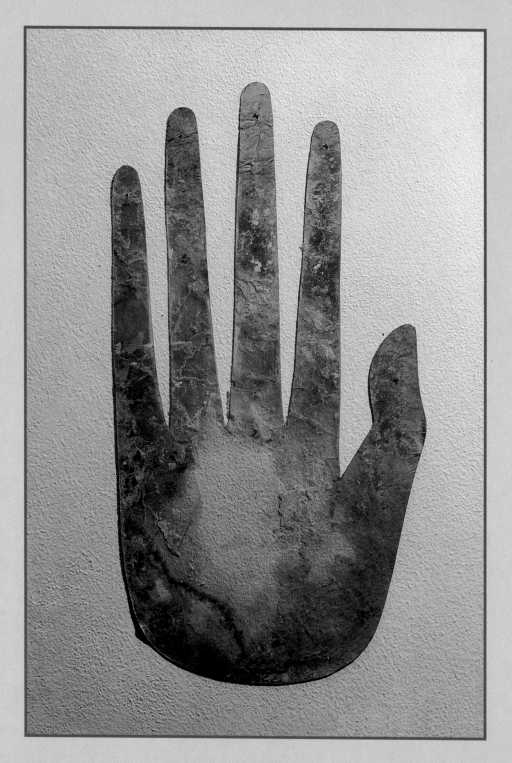

In many Native American tribes, the human hand is a powerful shaman's symbol. This one made of mica, a translucent mineral that forms in sheets, is a relic of the ancient Hopewell culture, which flourished in the region of present-day Ohio between 300 B.C. and A.D. 500.

continued from page 40

demonstrates the all-inclusiveness of the Navajo medical system:

> I have made your sacrifice.
> I have prepared a smoke for you.
> My feet restore for me.
> My legs restore for me.
> My body restore for me.
> My mind restore for me. . . .
> Impervious to pain, may I walk.
> Feeling light within, may I walk.
> With lively feelings, may I walk.
> Happily may I walk.
> Happily abundant dark clouds I desire.
> Happily abundant vegetation I desire.
> Happily abundant pollen I desire.
> Happily abundant dew I desire. . . .
> May it be happy before me.
> May it be happy behind me.
> May it be happy below me.
> May it be happy above me.
> With it happy all around me, may I walk.
> It is finished in beauty. . . .
> It is finished in beauty.

In some communities, healers are also expected to go into trances. It is believed that while in trances, healers can communicate directly with the spirit world to discover the cause of an ailment or the proper treatment of illness. It is both difficult and dangerous to enter a trance. The healer is aided by repetitive music, drum beating, and rhythmical singing and dancing, but because the trance involves contact with the spirit world, the danger persists. The spirits, far more knowledgeable and powerful than humans, are in control. Being in a trance state is also physically exhausting; healers may tremble, shake their bodies, faint, or appear detached from the physical world. One Kwakiutl healer describes the experience this way: "[A]ll the strength gathers in the stomach. The doctor has the feeling as though knives were cutting his insides."

In several regions of North America, Native American healers are organized into medicine societies that have several methods of recruiting members. People who are interested in becoming healers may apply to join and then become apprenticed to already practicing healers. In some cases, people become members of medicine societies after having been cured by a member; part of their cure or payment requires them to join. Some medicine societies add to their number by invitation: members approach the new recruit, who usually has little choice in the matter. To refuse membership is to risk angering the spirits who guide and protect the medicine society.

The Iroquois of the Northeast have six medicine societies, each specializing in treatments and ritual cures for particular ailments. The most important of the Iroquois medicine societies is the Society of Medicine Men. During curative rituals, each member sings a personal song revealed to him or her in visions and dreams. Another group is called the Little Water Society, and this society's most powerful medicine is comprised of various animal parts. A third group is the Company of Mystic Animals, a cluster of four related groups, each dedicated to the power of a specific animal: the Bear, Buffalo, Eagle, and Otter. Members of the Company of Mystic Animals

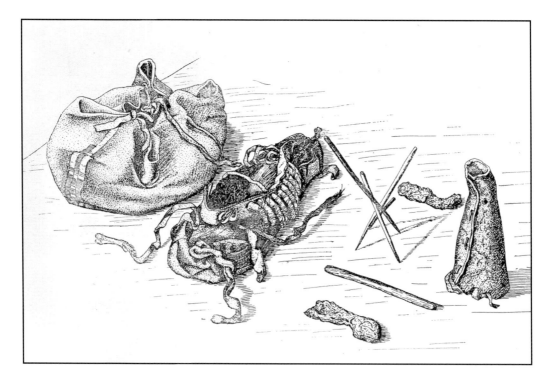

One of the sacred bags of the Arapaho "seven old women," shamans who used these sacred objects to supervise tipi embroidery and the decoration of buffalo robes and cradles. Prayers for health and long life accompanied the designs. Shown from left to right are the outer bag, holding gifts of food; an inner bag; two small bags of incense, called "man" and "woman"; a stick representing the gift of a horse; four small sticks arranged to represent a tipi; and a standing leather cone, the spirit of the bag itself.

perform ritual treatment in which they invoke these powers by imitating the actions, gait, and sounds of the animal to which the group is dedicated. The False Face Society and the Husk Face Society use masks when curing. The Society of Little People, said to be under the guidance of especially powerful spirit beings who are small in size, sings its healing songs in darkness and is often called the Dark Dance Society.

Among several native nations in the upper Midwest, healers are organized into a medical and religious organization called the Medicine Society or Medicine Lodge. Healers may seek membership themselves or they may be initiated after having been cured by a practicing doctor. Among the Dakota of Wisconsin and Minnesota, members of the Medicine Lodge are initiated into the organization through a group ritual. Each initiate is sponsored by an established member, usually a relative. Sponsors give novices medicine bags containing stones, birds, feathers, and animal bones that have spirit healing powers, and prospective healers must learn the medical and ritual cures used by lodge members.

After initiates learn the required curing prayers and songs, the rite of initiation, or "medicine dance," is held in a special lodge built in a clearing in the woods. The dance is observed by the entire community, beginning in the early morning. Initiates and members form two rows, one on each side of the lodge. Facing inward and holding their powerful medicine bags, dancers sing songs accompanied by constant drumming. The dramatic conclusion of one such medicine dance was described by Charles Eastman, a 19th-century Santee Dakota physician:

> The initiates were led out in front of the lodge and placed in a kneeling position upon a carpet of rich robes and fur, the men upon the right-hand, stripped and painted black, with a round spot of red just over the heart, while the women, dressed in their best, were arranged upon the left. Both sexes wore their hair loose, as if in mourning or expectation of death. An equal number of Society members, each appointed to one of the novices, faced them at a distance of perhaps fifty feet.
>
> The members assumed an attitude of dignity, crouching slightly, and grasping their medicine bags in both hands. Swinging their arms forward at the same moment, they uttered a cry in perfect unison, with startling effect. In the midst of a breathless silence, they stepped forward, ending a yard or so from the row of kneeling victims, with a mighty swing of the sacred bags that would seem to project all their mystic

A mask of the Iroquois False Face Society, one of six Iroquois medicine societies. As with other tribes, such as the Dakota and the Pueblo nations, each medicine society specializes in treatments and ritual cures for particular ailments.

> power into the bodies of the initiates. Instantly, the initiates all fell forward, apparently lifeless.

After having been "shot" with spirit power, the fallen initiates are covered with buffalo robes as though they are about to be buried. But they are "resurrected" shortly by the songs and prayers of society members. When initiates regain consciousness, they cough up a small shell or pebble from their mouths, then join the members in dancing and singing. This particular ritual, performed

Blackfeet men gather inside a medicine lodge and pass around a medicine pipe during a healing ceremony, while onlookers watch from outside the lodge. Native American healing rituals emphasize not only wholeness of mind and body, but also wholeness of the community in which the patient lives.

with minor variations by several Native American nations in the upper Midwest, is an enactment of the symbolic death and rebirth that members of powerful medicine societies must experience.

In the southwestern United States, Pueblo nations such as the Cochiti also have medicine societies. The number varies among Pueblo tribes. The Cochiti, located along the Rio Grande River in New Mexico, have five medicine societies: the Flint, the Fire Medicine Society, the Snake Society, the Giant Society, and a society whose native name is Poshai-ani. As with midwestern medicine societies, each has its own specialized ritual treatments. Cures are usually undertaken by the group as a whole, although in cases of minor illness one member's work might prove sufficient.

To join a healing society, Cochiti novices spend four years in training, during which time they fast periodically and abstain from sexual activity. At a preappointed time, all society members complete a four-day retreat to prepare for the candidates' initiation. After praying over the candidates, the members present them each with a "corn fetish," a perfect ear of blue corn to which bird feathers are attached. This fetish becomes an important element in the new healer's medicine kit.

All of the Cochiti medicine societies function together during rituals that mark the seasons of the year. In the springtime, for example, they plant prayer sticks in village irrigation ditches to bless the water and the seed-planting that will ultimately feed the community.

At other times of the year, the five Cochiti societies perform general cures for all residents of the village. Medicine societies in other Pueblo tribes, such as the Zuni, perform similar "overall" cures. These spectacular and dramatic rituals demonstrate and strengthen the supernatural powers that protect their members and endow them with knowledge. Members of the Zuni's Snake Medicine Society and Little Fire Society, for example, bathe in and swallow fire and dance on hot coals without injury. The Sword People immerse themselves in icy winter water and swallow swords and sticks and remain unharmed. Such dangerous and powerful rituals are thought to bless and cure the entire communities in which they are performed.

A Tlingit healer performs a curative rite over an ill man.

4

RITUAL HEALING

Beliefs about supernatural causes of illness vary among Native American groups. In some cultures, illness is thought to result from a patient's prior actions or from contact with harmful objects or forces, while in others, spirits are believed to inflict sickness as a punishment for wrongdoing. In some cultures, malevolent human witches or sorcerers are believed to cause illness. In all cultures, however, diagnosis of an ailment's cause is crucial to deciding on a course of treatment. Once a diagnosis is made, a healer can perform ceremonies to eliminate the underlying causative factors. Although most cures are effective, some treatments fail, leading to prolonged illness and eventual death. When this occurs, it is usually blamed on the healer's skills, which are considered too weak to counteract the supernatural forces that caused the disease.

The Inuit of the Canadian and American Arctic believe that illness sometimes results from actions that have offended supernatural beings. If men fail to honor properly the spirits of the animals they hunt or if women fail to abide by taboos during pregnancy, they may become ill. The same might happen if a person has been uncooperative, argumentative, or bad-tempered. When patients do not respond to simple treatments, the Inuit healer asks them to review their past behavior. If a patient recalls some wrongful act, he or she publicly admits the error, and the healer gives the patient rules to follow for a specified period of time. A patient may be told to abstain from eating certain foods or to throw away articles of clothing or household goods.

The Iroquois of the Northeast also believe that some illnesses result from people's thoughts and actions. However, their theory of disease stresses the role of an individual's inner wishes as a possible cause of ailments. They believe that

one's inner wishes are expressed in dreams and that one must satisfy these wishes to maintain good health. If people deny their own desires, they may become ill. Therefore, Iroquois healers ask patients to recall their dreams.

According to one description by 17th-century Jesuits living among Iroquoian peoples, dreams were believed by these Native Americans to be a primary indication of a person's illness. A dream might suggest the cause and

Edward S. Curtis's 1908 photograph Night Men Dancing—Arikara *depicts healers of the Medicine Fraternity, who perform spectacular healing feats such as standing on red hot stones and leaping through fire during night rituals. Such techniques are especially important when patients have difficulty determining the cause of their illness.*

treatment of illness, but it might also be the cause itself:

> One of the causes of disease is in the mind of the patient himself, which desires something, and will vex the body of the sick man until it possesses the thing required. For they think that there are in every man certain inborn desires, often unknown to themselves, upon which the happiness of individuals depends. For the purpose of ascertaining

Pueblo medicine men gather in their ceremonial chamber and invoke the power of their animal protector, the bear, to cure a boy of a sore throat.

desires and innate appetites of this character, they summon soothsayers, who, as they think, have a divinely imparted power to look into the inmost recesses of the mind.

These innate appetites or desires were often revealed to people only in their dreams. The soothsayers, or fortune-tellers, were skilled healers who interpreted the content of people's dreams and recommended treatment.

In some cases, the wishes expressed in dreams are overt and obvious. For example, a patient may remember dreaming about receiving a particular present, visiting with a relative or friend, or attending a specific kind of ceremony. When this occurs, members of the community attempt to satisfy the patient's wishes by presenting the desired gift, arranging for the relative or friend to visit, or performing the desired ceremony.

In cases where the patient's wish is not so obvious, the patient seeks the aid of a healer who specializes in determining hidden desires. These healers use a number of ritual techniques to receive messages from the spirit realm concerning the patient's wish, including gazing into water or fire, fasting, or entering a trance in an attempt to see images of the desire. Once the wish has been determined, the patient and his or her family try to fulfill it.

Several Native American theories of disease are based on the belief that an illness can result from the loss of an individual's soul. According to the Inuit, the soul normally leaves the body during sleep and returns just before the sleeper awakens. If a soul does not come back because it is lost or because it has been captured or harmed by evil spirits or witches, the individual will become gravely ill and will eventually die. Symptoms of soul loss include a depletion of energy and appetite, insomnia, and depression. These cases must be dealt with swiftly in order to save the patient's life.

A patient suffering from soul loss is treated by a spiritual healer called an *angakot,* who attempts to retrieve the lost soul by using a dramatic and emotionally intense ritual. This ritual occurs at night in a darkened house, where all of the lights are extinguished and the windows and doorways are covered. Family and community members gather before the patient, who lies on a mat. The angakot takes a place behind the patient and summons spiritual helpers—cooperative souls of ghosts, animals, and supernatural beings that the angakot has acquired over the years through prayers, dreams, and other spiritual means. After singing and drumming for a period of time, the angakot enters a trance and speaks to these helpers in a special language, commanding them to join the healer on a spirit journey to seek the patient's lost soul. Along the way, they encounter evil creatures trying to block their path, and they must fight these creatures in order to locate and rescue the lost soul. Patients and their families can often hear the loud shouts and moans of the angakot, the helpers, and the malicious creatures during these battles. At the end of a successful ritual cure, the angakot retrieves the patient's soul and returns it to the body. Patients usually experience feelings of tremendous emotional relief when their souls are returned to them, and recovery from the illness quickly follows.

Among the Kwakiutl of British Columbia, soul loss was also believed to be a common cause of disease. A Kwakiutl healer describes a typical procedure performed in the late 19th and early 20th centuries:

> I went to look after the soul of a patient. I went around the fire, carrying my rattle and singing my sacred song. During this time the patient had to sit up in the rear of the house, his hands on his knees. Then I felt the crown of his head and said that the soul was absent. I told his father to throw clothing, food, and oil into the fire, and to ask for the help of the spirit of the fire. This induced the souls to come to the house. They quarreled among themselves for possession of the clothing and food. As soon as the souls appeared, I ran about looking for the soul of the patient. Suddenly I caught the soul in my hand.
>
> I showed it on my hands and walked around the fire four times. Then I swallowed it, saying that I was going to blow it into the patient's head. I stood at the door, holding the soul between the palms of my hands. Then I walked up to the patient, opened my hands, and

These tiny fiber and bone figurines, each less than three inches high, were used by shamans during healing rituals to represent the illnesses that they would suck from the bodies of their patients.

blew upon them. I stepped up to the patient, pressed my hands on the crown of his head, and blew upon it. Thus I put the soul back into the sick person, whose body it filled at once.

Many Native American peoples believe that disease can be caused by the intrusion of foreign objects, particles, or substances into human bodies and that these objects must be located and extracted in order to restore health. These foreign objects are believed to disrupt the inner physical and psychic harmony and balance necessary to good health. Supernatural beings may shoot these objects into a victim's body as punishment for failing to show respect to the spirits or neglecting ritual rules. Human witches also shoot objects into someone to retaliate for a real or imagined slight.

Shoshone and Comanche healers of the western Plains have several techniques for extracting foreign objects hidden in a patient's body. Disease-causing objects include tiny feathers, pebbles, bits of animal bone, and a special liquid substance without particular shape, and they produce a variety of symptoms, such as localized pain, swelling, or stiffness. Healers often begin by gently massaging the afflicted area. Then they remove the object by sucking on the spot. Once retrieved, the object is spat out and thrown into a fire or otherwise ritually purified and discarded.

The following description of a Cree ritual performed to extract harmful objects was recorded in the early 19th century:

> At length, old Mukkwah [the healer] said he heard the sound of bad fire in the breast of the patient, and putting one hand to his breast, and his mouth to the back, he continued sometime blowing and rubbing, when he, as if by accident, dropped a little ball on the ground. He at length threw it into the fire, where it burned, with a little whizzing noise, like damp powder. Then he said that there was a snake in the breast of the sick man which he could not remove till the following day, when with similar preparation, and similar mummeries, he seemed to draw out of the body of the sick man, a small snake.

Some Native American peoples, including the Apache of the American Southwest, believe that certain forces of nature are dangerous and powerful and can cause illness if an unprotected person comes into contact with them. For the Apache, one of the most likely disease-causing forces is lightning. If people are in the presence of lightning or if they touch a tree or house that has been struck by lightning, they may become ill. In such cases, a ceremony is performed to erase or counteract the harmful effects. This ritual cure is described as follows:

> Towards dusk friends and relatives [of the patient] started to arrive. Soon it was dark and someone started a fire. The healer was on hand. All was in readiness.
>
> It is well past midnight, and the healer has been chanting steadily for over two hours. The chant, which comes from the "Lightning" corpus is high pitched and intricate in tempo. The beat of the drums is steady, almost monotonous. Standing behind the healer and drummers are ten or twelve men who joined in the chorus which follows each verse. They are not medicine men, these additional singers, nor do they necessarily own a power.

The chant comes to an end. The healer rises and walks away. The midpoint in the ceremony has been reached, and now it is time for everyone to rest and eat. It is close to three o'clock when the curing ceremonial resumes. The fire is replenished. Once again the healer and the drummers take their places. The chants begin again.

With the first light of dawn, the singing stops. Picking up a small basket filled with cattail pollen, the healer walks to where Clinton [the patient] is sitting. He sprinkles pollen on each of Clinton's shoulders and on the top of his head. Next he takes from the basket a piece of "lightning grass" and touches it to Clinton's forehead. This action, it is

Members of the Zuni Galaxy Fraternity during a ritual healing ceremony. As in many other Native American medicine societies, those cured during the ceremony were then initiated into the society.

believed, will neutralize the "lightning power" in Clinton's brain. The pollen blessing is then repeated. The healer returns to his seat and sings two final chants. The ceremonial is over, and people prepare to leave. Clinton gets up from his pile of blankets and walks slowly to his hut. He lies down on his bed and goes instantly to sleep.

Like the Apache, the Navajo also believe that people can become sick if they have had contact with a contaminating object, being, or force. Numerous animals, insects, and plants can potentially cause illness, including bears, porcupines, coyotes, rattlesnakes, ants, moths, and cacti. Natural forces such as lightning and whirlwinds are also dangerous. The

Navajo theory of contamination is based on the belief that health requires the maintenance of internal and external balances. Certain objects, animals, and natural forces cause disruptions in a person's normal balance that lead to disease if not properly counteracted. Consequently, treatments are aimed at removing the harmful effects of contamination and restoring the body to its normal state of harmony and beauty.

Another Native American theory of disease (often found in conjunction with the theories mentioned above) maintains that illness and other misfortunes can be caused by witches or sorcerers. Witches and sorcerers are humans who perform harmful magic because they are malicious, aggressive, jealous, and spiteful. They magically attack people who have slighted them, and since they are jealous and oversensitive, they may do evil against innocent people who have caused them no harm.

Each culture has different beliefs about how witches practice their arts. In general, they are thought to have access to supernatural powers that they acquire through prayers, visions, and dreams. They can also learn witchcraft from other practitioners, paying fees for their apprenticeship. In all cases, witches work in secret, since any society that accepts their existence also has very strong prohibitions about the practice of witchcraft and will persecute anyone who is proven to be a witch.

In many societies, people believe that witches may also be healers, because the supernatural powers that enable people to cure disease are essentially neutral and can be used for malicious purposes as well as good. The Skokomish of western Washington believe that healers (called doctors) can be responsible for both health and illness. If doctors want to harm someone, they may shoot foreign objects into the victim or extract the victim's life-soul. One Skokomish gave an account of an evil doctor's practice:

> Doctors used their powers to kill people by shooting sticks into them, or they'd go to people when they were sleeping and draw their life-soul out of them, pull it out of their heads, and hide it in the graveyard. Or they'd wrap the life-soul in cedar bark and hang it in the smoke of the fire in their houses and make you awful sick and kill you. It was dangerous to shoot doctor power into a person, because another doctor might find it there and kill it, and that would kill the doctor that sent it.
>
> A big chief was dying, and they sent there and got Duke Williams [a healer] to doctor him. And Duke found that man's life-soul all wrapped up in cedar bark and hanging in another man's house. And he brought it back with his spirit power, and washed it and put it back in the sick man, and that man got well.

The Apache believe that witches have several techniques for causing illness and death. They may use poisons made from the skin of human corpses, bear feces, rattlesnake skin, and bits of wood taken from trees that have been struck by lightning. These poisons are put into victims' food, thrown into their

This engraving depicts an 18th-century Native American healing ceremony during which malign creatures, such as the winged demon portrayed above the lodge, are driven from the ailing person's body and soul.

This 1905 drawing by a Seneca artist depicts members of the False Face Society during a ceremony known as the Traveling Rite. Held each spring and fall, the ritual purified and protected tribal homes from illness.

houses, or dropped into their noses or mouths while they sleep. Witches can also cause illness by uttering malicious spells or by thinking evil thoughts about their victims. Like spirits, they may shoot harmful objects into victims' bodies. The following Apache narrative illustrates such an incident:

> That time I was with X and we were working on the drift fence near that spotted mountain. At night, that time, X was by the fire eating his grub. He said to me, "I don't feel so good." Then he went to sleep. In the night he woke up and said, "I was just sleeping there and I wake up with big pain right here, here in my neck. It sure hit me all of a sudden." Then that time later in the night, it hit him again. He said, "I wonder who is shooting at me?" Then I know that someone is after him with shooting sorcery.

When ailments come on suddenly, witchcraft is usually suspected. Witchcraft is also considered at fault if an illness does not respond to usual ritual treatments or if several people in a family get sick or die within a short period of time. Apaches who suffer from ailments caused by witchcraft are treated by rituals that remove the harmful spell and restore good health. If the cure successfully leads to the patient's recovery, the witch responsible will become ill from the same malady and die soon afterward.

Native American beliefs in supernatural causes and treatments of illness have a common theme. People appeal to the spirit world to learn the reasons for life and death and ways of coping with problems over which they seemingly have little control. Curing rituals express people's desire to understand their fate, a truth succinctly expressed by a Navajo healer who was asked whether a patient cured of an illness by a Red Ant Chantway actually had ants in his body. The healer replied, "No, not ants, but *ants*. We have to have a way of thinking strongly about disease." Imagining illnesses as tangible things— animals, plants, or other creatures— helps both healer and patient understand and take steps to cure them.

Native American healing rituals are effective in other ways as well. They provide reassurance for the patient and stress the community's involvement and concern with his or her good health. During a curative ritual, statements such as "I am healing you, I am curing you," or "you are getting well, you are being cured" are repeated often by the healer to express a strong belief in the patient's ability to recover. Moreover, because such rituals are public events in which friends, relatives, and other community members participate, the patient becomes the center of attention of the whole community and feels valued and loved. In this way, ritual cures address the spiritual and psychological contributors to disease and help to relieve patients of the anxiety, tension, and feelings of loneliness and helplessness that can accompany and exacerbate many physical complaints. Throughout each ritual treatment, the patient is encouraged to look forward to a successful cure and to be restored in body, mind, and spirit.

The French explorer Jacques Cartier. European travelers to North America were often surprised to learn that Native Americans had already developed remedies for many of the ailments that afflicted the explorers.

5

LEARNING FROM NATIVE AMERICAN MEDICINE

In 1536 the French explorer Jacques Cartier landed near Quebec, Canada, to survey the northeastern region of North America. Soon after arriving, however, 25 of his crew members died of scurvy, a disease now known to be caused by a deficiency of vitamin C in the diet. At that time, Europeans had no cure for this potentially fatal ailment, but the Native Americans they encountered, known as the Laurentian Iroquois, had discovered a treatment. One of Cartier's officers describes the Europeans' surprise upon learning that a remedy was available:

> One day our captain, seeing the disease so general and his men so stricken down by it caught sight of a band of Indians approaching from Stadacona (Quebec), and among them was Domagaya whom he had seen ten days previous to this, extremely ill with the very disease his own men were suffering from; for one of his legs above the knee had swollen to the size of a two year old

baby, and the sinews had become contracted. His teeth had gone bad and decayed, and the gums had rotted and become tainted. The Captain, seeing Domagaya well was delighted, hoping to learn what had healed him, in order to cure his own men. And when the Indians had come near the fort, the Captain inquired of him, what had cured him of his sickness. Domagaya replied that he had been healed by the juice of the leaves of a tree and the dregs of these, and that this was the only way to cure sickness. Upon this the Captain asked him to show it to him that he might heal his servant who in his opinion had caught the disease, being unwilling that he should know how many sailors were ill. Thereupon Domagaya sent two women with our Captain to gather some of it; and they brought back nine or ten branches. They showed us how to grind the bark and the leaves and to boil the whole in water. . . . According to them this tree cured every kind of disease. They call it in their language Annedda.

A stand of white pine in Menominee territory in Wisconsin. As with hundreds of botanicals, the bark and leaves of white pine have been used by Native Americans as a curative since at least the 16th century, when one of Jacques Cartier's officers described with amazement how the natives they encountered were able to cure scurvy.

The tree that the natives used was the hemlock, or white pine. The Laurentian Iroquois and members of other Iroquois nations also drank hemlock tea as a preventive remedy during the winter. Their success in healing Cartier's sailors provides a vivid illustration of Native American willingness to impart medical knowledge to European explorers, travelers, missionaries, and settlers on their land. Most Europeans, recognizing the value of the natural remedies that native people had developed, readily availed themselves of the knowledge and skills of the indigenous peoples they encountered.

Dramatic instances of successful treatments of nonnative Americans and Canadians by traditional healers are documented in the 20th century as well. For example, the prestigious British medical journal *Lancet* reported in 1904 on an effective treatment by a Native American healer in the Canadian province of Manitoba. The incident concerned a railway worker with an injured hand, whose condition was complicated by blood poisoning. The young Canadian worker had accidentally driven a nail through the palm of his hand, and it had become increasingly swollen and painful. On the way to a medical doctor 70 miles away, he came upon a Native American camp on the Manitoba prairies, where he received treatment from a traditional healer. The *Lancet* reported:

> The old woman [the healer] took the wounded hand in hers and gently rubbed her other hand to and fro over the swelling and up and down on the whole arm, all the while chanting a weird song. At the same time all of the other women took up the chant and forming themselves into a circle walked round and round the two during the whole operation. The young fellow's mind was so acted upon by the effect of the mysterious chanting that his attention was entirely taken away from the pain he was suffering, which, of course, was the real object of the strange performance. He became

so hot that he fell into a perfuse perspiration, and when the woman was satisfied with the results of her treatment she made a poultice from some particular leaves elected for such purposes and bounded over the hand, the Indians then carried the patient into the inner part of the tent where he was laid down and covered with skins, here he slept for eighteen hours. When he awoke the pain and swelling had entirely gone from his arm and being now in a more fit state to complete the remainder of his journey he went on to the doctor and told him his experience. The doctor was so satisfied with what had been done that he said if the patient had not undergone treatment of the old woman he would have had to lose his arm.

Although the account does not identify the plants used by the Native healer to treat the swelling and infection in the worker's hand, it exemplifies how ritual and natural treatments used by healers could be combined to effect cures.

Today, in many rural parts of the United States and Canada, both Native American and other patients turn to traditional healers for relief from illness and pain. Cherokee healers in North Carolina report that they are often visited by outsiders whose medical doctors have advised them that their conditions are incurable. Whether or not the healers are able to cure such patients, it is important that their aid is sought. Such actions speak not merely of a patient's wish to survive but also of the high regard that those in need of treatment still hold for Native American healers.

As we have seen, Native American remedies were adopted by North American medical practitioners as early as the 17th century. European doctors often relied on traditional Native American medicines to treat their own patients. Some of these remedies eventually became part of the standard American pharmacopoeia, and nonnative practitioners sometimes called themselves "Indian" doctors. One 19th-century doctor named Peter Smith compiled a book of remedies entitled *The Indian Doctor's Dispensatory, Being Father Smith's Advice Respecting Diseases and Their Cure*, in which he wrote:

> I call myself an "Indian Doctor" because I have obtained a knowledge of many of the simples [remedies] used by the Indians; but chiefly because I have obtained my knowledge generally in the like manner the Indians do. I have by continued observation come to be of the opinion that our best medicines grow in the woods and gardens.

Although many of the "patent medicines" that became popular during the American colonial period did not contain actual Native American remedies, they often capitalized on the popularity of these treatments. Many were named—and advertised—as "Indian" cures. As early as 1711, a patent medicine touted as a cure for tuberculosis was called "Tuscarora Rice" after the Tuscarora, a Virginia Iroquois nation. In the 19th century, patent medicines grew increasingly popular and continued to be named for Native American tribes,

even though in most cases no actual connection existed between the tribe and the remedy. Preparations like "Modoc Oil," "Seminole Cough Balsam," and "Wonderworking Kickapoo Indian Prairie Plant" contained none of the curative substances of the tribes named; the purveyors simply took advantage of the popular belief in the effectiveness of Native American cures.

A number of authentic Native American remedies were so widely adopted by nonnatives that they became important trade items in America and abroad. The earliest of these was sassafras, a northeastern laurel tree commonly called the "universal plant" because its leaves and roots were effective in curing a wide array of ailments. Its use among the Iroquois was described by Jesuit missionaries in the 17th century:

> [Sassafras] leaves which are as broad as one's hand, have the shape of the lily as depicted in heraldry; and its roots have the smell of the laurel. The most vivid scarlet, the brightest green, the most natural yellow and orange of Europe pale before the various colors that the Onondaga procure from its roots.

Sassafras was used by native people in many ways: as a blood purifier, a treatment for rheumatism, a diuretic, and a tonic taken after childbirth. After learning about its healing properties from southeastern natives, 16th-century Spanish settlers began shipping large quantities to Spain for distribution throughout Europe. The demand for sassafras grew so quickly that expeditions

A female shaman cures a European settler of a snakebite. As early as the 17th century, North American medical practitioners were adopting Native American remedies and methods to treat their own patients. Today, many nonnative patients continue to seek relief from traditional healers.

were launched specifically to collect and export the plant to Europe. As the number of European settlers in North America increased, the uses of sassafras grew beyond traditional applications; Swedish immigrants in New Jersey, for example, began putting sassafras peels in their beer and claimed that it was also an effective insecticide for moths and bedbugs. Women in Philadelphia, Pennsylvania, used sassafras to make an orange dye for woolen cloth.

Another Native American remedy widely exported from North America to Europe was maidenhair fern, which had been employed by Iroquois women to ease labor pains and was used as a general treatment for coughs and other respiratory

This 1905 advertisement for a hair remedy illustrates how "patent medicines" that did not contain actual Native American remedies nevertheless capitalized on the popularity of such treatments.

ailments. By the late 17th century, maidenhair fern, like sassafras, had become an important export item. An 18th-century observer noted the reasons for its popularity among Europeans:

> Several people in Albany and Canada assured [me] that its leaves were very much used instead of tea in consumption, cough, and all kinds of pectoral diseases.

This they have learned from the Indians who have made use of the plant for these purposes since ancient times. This American maidenhair is reckoned preferable in surgery to that which we have in Europe and therefore they send a great quantity of it to France every year.

Ginseng, a perennial herb with scarlet berries and aromatic roots, was another widely exported plant in colonial America. The earliest shipments were sent to China via France and England; direct export routes to China were established by the end of the 18th century. The plant became so popular in Europe and China that overcollection nearly eradicated it within a few decades after exportation began. Today, ginseng is still a well-known curative in China.

More than 170 substances derived from plants that have been used by native peoples of North America—including roots, flowers, bulbs, tubers, trees, leaves, herbs, berries, fruits, nuts, seeds, and mints—have been officially listed as drugs in the *Pharmacopeia of the United States of America* and the *National Formulary*. Many retain their original uses, while others have been adapted for purposes other than those of the Native Americans who first used them as curatives. For example, the Penobscots of Maine traditionally made poultices from the leaves of the white cedar tree to treat swollen hands and feet. The Ojibwa of the Great Lakes region drank a decoction of the leaves to purify the blood and ease coughing, and the Montagnai of northern Quebec mashed the ends of white cedar twigs and steeped them in a tea to relieve heart pains. In the *National Formulary*, although white cedar twigs are recommended for use as a diuretic (which often relieves swelling), they are also named as a stimulant. Similarly, dandelion roots, used by the Ojibwa to relieve heartburn and by the Meskwaki to counteract chest pains, are also listed in the official drug registers as a diuretic. Hops, a wild plant growing in eastern and central North America and used by the Ojibwa, Menominee, and Dakota for fevers, intestinal pains, and congestion in the lungs, gained official recognition for use as a bitter tonic and a sedative.

Nonbotanical substances were also adopted by standard medical practitioners in the United States. For example, alum, a mineral used mainly as an astringent, was used by Native Americans at least as early as the 16th century. A 16th-century European settler observed that alum was "found by some of our physicians to bee of the same kinde of vertue and more effectuall [than similar substances commonly used in Europe]. The inhabitants use it very much for the cure of sores and woundes: there is in divers places great plentie, and in some places of a blewe sort."

Another such substance was charcoal, traditionally used in a pulverized form to stop nosebleeds. Charcoal derived from wood was also taken as a tea for bowel and stomach complaints. Some tribes, such as the Tewa of New Mexico, drank an infusion of hot water and charcoal to relieve coughs and sore throats. Petroleum, a coal derivative first discovered in precontact times by the Seneca of the Northeast, was noted by 18th-century French settlers to cure toothaches, headaches, rheumatism, and injured joints.

Undoubtedly the most well-known plant borrowed from Native Americans is tobacco. Although Europeans and early American settlers hailed tobacco as a panacea, or cure-all, indigenous people used it only sparingly as medicine. New England natives treated burns and scalds

The white cedar tree is one of the more than 170 botanicals used by Native Americans that have been officially listed as drugs in the Pharmacopeia of the United States of America *and the* National Formulary.

The image of a figure smoking a huge pipe in this 16th-century engraving of the nicotiana (or tobacco) plant illustrates its vast popularity among European settlers both as a medicinal and recreational drug.

with a wash made of boiled tobacco leaves, and the Mohican and Malecite of the Northeast blew tobacco smoke into the ear to cure earaches. In the Southeast, the Creek and Choctaw treated stomach cramps with a weak tobacco tea, while Mississippi natives applied tobacco to external abscesses and inflammations.

Among Native American tribes, the tobacco plant was used primarily for ceremonial purposes. The Iroquois burned tobacco offerings to spirit beings in the belief that the smoke carried their messages to the supernatural realm. Many Eastern and Plains natives smoked tobacco in pipes on ritual occasions as offerings to spirit beings, during ceremonial preparations, and when concluding negotiations and councils.

Europeans, on the other hand, viewed tobacco primarily as a medicinal substance. Beginning in the 16th century, tobacco was used to relieve headaches, coughs, stomachaches, toothaches, convulsions, malaria, worms, dropsy, lockjaw, nasal allergies, bee sting pain, and abscesses of the skin. While medical claims for tobacco increased, smoking the plant for recreational purposes in pipes and in cigarette form became popular as well.

Not all Europeans believed that the tobacco plant was a "wonder drug." King James I of England issued a scathing condemnation of the practice of smoking the plant:

> [It is] a custome lothsome to the eye, hatefull to the nose, harmefull to the braine, dangerous to the lungs, and in the blacke stinking fume thereof, nearest resembling the horrible Stigian smoke of the pit that is bottomlesse.

Despite such dire warnings, tobacco smoking grew enormously popular. Tobacco production for domestic and international sale became the economic backbone of several early American colonies, especially Virginia, the Carolinas, and Maryland. Today, of course, we know that smoking or chewing tobacco is detrimental to one's health, despite the health claims of earlier centuries.

The contrast between Native American uses of tobacco and those of Europeans and American settlers illustrates the philosophical differences in health practices between the two groups. The commonly held Native American belief in moderation was applied to tobacco use; the plant was used mainly as a ritual substance and in highly restricted contexts, thus reducing the risk of ill effects from habitual use. Europeans and American settlers, however, used tobacco much more broadly and indulged in it daily. They were prone, then, to the serious health problems that often accompany overuse.

Other cultures can learn valuable lessons about health methods and practices from Native Americans. Moderation in activities and diet, avoiding harmful substances and actions, and cleansing the body both externally and internally are among the many ways that Native American peoples strive to stay healthy and to hasten their recovery from illness. Native American medicine also teaches that emotional and social well-being are essential to physical health. The body, the mind, the spirit, and the environment in which people live are all addressed with remedies that treat the living being as a total system made of many parts and in complete harmony with its environment.

A peyote drummer. The intense visions experienced after ingesting pieces of the cactus are believed to come from spirit beings. Native American peyote ceremonies originated during the late 19th century and are still performed today in many parts of the United States.

6

TRADITION
AND CHANGE

In many ways, Native American medicine has changed significantly since the arrival of Europeans in North America more than 500 years ago. Natural remedies and ritual treatments used by healers in precontact times are still used today in some communities, but the percentage of Native Americans who seek traditional treatment has greatly diminished. Ceremonial cures in particular are mostly restricted to Native American communities that retain their traditions and culture. Even in such societies, some residents may no longer follow these practices.

In some tribes or groups, traditional healing systems have evolved to incorporate medicines borrowed from other cultures. Also, because the demand for traditional healing remedies and rituals has dwindled, modern medical techniques have largely replaced the ceremonial surgical procedures for removing intrusive objects, treating broken bones, and extracting teeth. Although some communities still practice ceremonial cures,

in many others the process has been replaced by visits to medical doctors and hospitals.

The primary causes of these changes occurred soon after Europeans first arrived in the New World. Religious and ideological conversions began slowly. In the 17th and 18th centuries, most Native American people remained faithful to their own beliefs regarding religion and medicine. Indeed, they had ample reason to continue traditional medical practices, since those healing techniques were at least as effective as those of Europeans. In fact, some Native American skills exceeded those of their Euroamerican contemporaries and were acknowledged by European testimonials.

The introduction of European diseases into native populations created medical chaos among indigenous communities. At first, healers tried to cope with the ravages of new conditions such as smallpox, measles, and influenza by using familiar and proven remedies,

Father Jacques Marquette, the Jesuit priest who accompanied Louis Jolliet in the race to beat English explorers to the Mississippi River in 1672, converses with the Native Americans whom the French encountered on the expedition. As European diseases spread through indigenous populations and missionary activity increased, the number of Native Americans converted to Christianity rose steadily.

but these often did little good or failed completely. At the same time, missionaries and other European agents campaigned vigorously—often using physical force or threats—to convince natives to adopt Christianity and abandon what the Europeans believed were primitive religions. Because medicine and religion are intimately connected in Native American belief systems, successful conversions of natives to Christianity threatened the very foundation of aboriginal theories of health, illness, and healing.

European missionaries took advantage of this philosophical breakdown to persuade Native Americans to abandon all of their traditional medical-religious belief systems and practices. Although Europeans attested to the effectiveness of Native American medicines and did not oppose their use, the missionaries objected vehemently to the rituals and procedures that often accompanied the cures. They felt that the religious beliefs on which such curative powers were based would inhibit the spread of Christianity among Native Americans. Thus the missionaries attacked the practice of ceremonial cures.

As European diseases spread throughout indigenous populations and death rates mounted, Native Americans sought solutions from nontradtional sources—including Christian missionaries. Christianity often attracted the most converts in areas where the incidence of smallpox, measles, and other deadly diseases was highest. For example, the Huron of Ontario accepted baptism from French Jesuit missionaries in the mistaken belief that it might cure smallpox. Although the baptismal rite could not cure people or protect them from death, many Huron tribe members viewed the rite as a final attempt to survive, in much the same way that they believed in other supernatural protections against illness. Because most Europeans seemed immune to the ravages of such diseases, the Huron assumed that they must have been protected by powerful spirits.

During the 17th and 18th centuries, the numbers of Native American conversions to Christianity steadily increased as disease rates rose and missionary activity spread. By the 19th century, American and Canadian officials, missionaries, and teachers had begun exerting even greater pressures on Native Americans to abandon their traditional beliefs and systems and assimilate themselves into Western culture. Gradually, as newer and more effective scientific techniques became known, Native American healers and community members began taking advantage of the benefits offered by these innovations.

The adoption of new medical practices did not eradicate traditional beliefs entirely, however. Most Native American systems were kept but were adapted to accommodate the new information. For example, the Iroquois expanded their medical remedies to include plants that had been introduced by Europeans, such as hartweed, mallows, yellow dock, Queen Anne's lace, catnip, and peppermint. The tribe also borrowed medicinal herbs, including common yarrow, mayweed, tansy, and burdock. One European, Peter Kalm, described the Iroquois adoption of the plantain herb in 1748:

> This plant was found in many places. Whether it was an original American plant or whether the Europeans had brought it over was in some doubt. This doubt had its rise from the natives (who always had an extensive knowledge of the plants of the country) saying that this plant never grew here before the arrival of the white men. They therefore gave it a name which signified the "Englishman's foot," for they say that wherever a European had walked, this plant grew in his footsteps.

Other remedies came not from imported plants but from other regions of North America. The most historically and culturally significant of these is peyote, a cactus that originated in Mexico, where it had been used for centuries by aboriginal peoples in religious ceremonies.

A group of Menominee seated around a Dream Dance drum. In the 1880s, the Dream Dance—a religion that combined Christian elements and traditional Menominee ways—was embraced by many Menominee who felt threatened by the changes brought to the reservation by non-Indians.

Peyote was first introduced to the southern Plains region by the Comanche and Kiowa around 1870. In North America, peyote ceremonies were performed both for religious and healing purposes. Its popularity spread throughout the West during the early 20th century. Today, it is commonly used by many Native American groups in the United States and Canada, with the exception of those east of the Mississippi River and among the Pueblo nations of the Southwest, where it is rarely, if ever, used.

Peyote is an hallucinogen—legal only on Native American reservations—that is believed to have both spiritual and healing properties. Participants in peyote rituals experience intense visions after ingesting pieces of the cactus. Believers view peyote as a spiritual agent that allows one to come into contact with strong supernatural powers and receive visions and messages from spirit beings.

Peyote rituals begin at sundown and continue through the night, ending at sunrise on the following day. A "road chief" supplies the peyote and leads ceremonial prayers and songs. Participants are seated in a circle and take turns playing a drum and singing personal songs that have come to them in visions and dreams. Each person consumes a peyote button taken from a plate that is passed around, after which the individual may begin to have visions and other spiritually meaningful experiences.

As a healing agent, peyote is used in several ways. Because one of its physical effects is to relax muscles and relieve pain, it is sometimes used as a means of easing difficult child labor. A peyote tea infusion is also a home remedy for mild or temporary illnesses. In serious cases, a patient will attend a peyote meeting to seek a cure.

Peyote occasionally causes indigestion or nausea. For this reason, it is believed to be especially effective for people suffering from the intrusion of foreign objects into their bodies. After ingesting peyote buttons, the patient typically vomits and is understood to have ejected the underlying cause of illness. During the treatment, those attending the ceremony pray for the patient's recovery and for renewed strength.

Just as Native American practitioners have adopted nontraditional plants and herbs, they have also included in their medicine kits many objects borrowed from European culture. In some cases, they have even replaced traditional equivalents. For instance, the Comanche healer Sanapia uses commercial mouthwash to rinse out her mouth before and after she performs ritual treatments involving the extraction of foreign objects. The mouthwash is used to "kill the poison" that touches her mouth during sucking treatments. Also, although Sanapia follows traditional Comanche curing practices, she uses a Christian Bible in some of her cures. Just as the eagle spirits provide guidance, knowledge, and protection, Sanapia believes that the Bible also holds healing power:

> I really read bible lots, and I go by the bible when I'm doctoring too. I always ask God to give power to my hands

A United States Coast Guard dentist examines an Inuit child at a remote Alaskan settlement. Greater acceptance of Western medical practices by Native Americans has been part of the process of their adopting mainstream American culture.

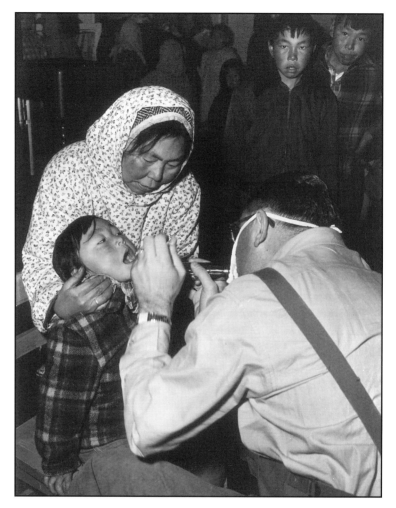

and mind. I pray hard to the Holy Ghost. My mother didn't go by the bible when she [was] doctoring, but I do, because you got to ask God for help sometimes.

This merging of Christian imagery and traditional beliefs is relatively common among Native American healers. A Cherokee healer in North Carolina describes a similar practice:

When I conjure, I go by the word of God. In ceremonies, I use the name of the Lord. When somebody sick, you take him to the creek, wash his face by dipping with your hand, and wet his breast by the heart. It's like the spirit gives strength, like baptism. He can feel it. If somebody's lost, it's up to the Creator to point the way. Sort of like in prayer. If it wasn't in the power of the Creator, you couldn't make anything move.

As with many religious beliefs and medical practices, time has also changed the way Native Americans interpret the symptoms and causes of illness. During the 19th century, Cherokee healers recited a prayer formula to counteract what they described as "something . . . causing something to eat them," which was manifested by fright and agitation on the part of the afflicted one. It was believed to result from the actions of one of four disease-causing spirits that gnawed at the patient's vital organs. Today, although the same prayer formula is used, it is recited only "when anyone takes faint or when his heart stops," a condition caused by a "weak heart or high blood pressure."

The relationship between one's dreams and one's health has also undergone reinterpretation. Among Huron, Iroquois, and Cherokee in the 17th and 18th centuries, dreams were understood to contain messages concerning a person's inner wishes; those which were unfulfilled could cause disease. Likewise, it was thought that patients were capable of dreaming the appropriate treatment to alleviate their conditions. Today, dreams are most often interpreted as omens of the future.

Native Americans on the whole have adopted much of "mainstream" American culture over the centuries since Europeans first arrived in North America. Greater acceptance of Western medical practices has been one part of this process. Today it is common for most Native Americans to seek conventional medical treatment for injuries, broken bones, and serious wounds, as well as for illnesses that native remedies do not seem to heal. On the other hand, traditional practitioners are still consulted for ailments that doctors and hospital care fail to cure.

Conflicts sometimes occur when different treatments are recommended by the two medical systems. One Cherokee healer questioned a conventional medical treatment for kidney trouble:

> Something juicy on the vine like a peach or a watermelon, the Indian doctor says no [forbids a patient to eat such fruit]. Doctors here in the hospital give orange juice and grapefruit, and it makes you worse, it hurts. Anything that swells up, you shouldn't take juice, only something dry or heavy.

In general, Native Americans who most closely adhere to traditional customs, beliefs, and languages are more likely to follow the advice of Native American practitioners, while those who are more assimilated into mainstream culture tend to seek Western medical solutions.

The percentages of all Native Americans who seek Western medical care have increased markedly during the 20th century. One reason is that hospital care on Native American reservations has greatly improved. A second reason is that, until recently, Native Americans rarely resorted to hospital care until traditional treatments had failed and they were near death. Because such care was often administered too late, many who entered hospitals did not survive. That

Susan La Flesche (center right), the daughter of an Omaha chief named Iron Eyes, was the embodiment of the growing relationship between Native American and Western healing practices. In 1889, she became the first Native American woman licensed in the United States as a physician. After earning her degree, she practiced among her own people and raised the funds to build a community hospital before her death in 1915.

observation led many Native Americans to avoid hospitals completely, in the mistaken belief that they caused death. As the quality of hospital care has improved, survival rates have risen and Native Americans have grown less averse to visiting a hospital in the first place.

Some of the best studies of Native Americans' use of traditional and Western medicine have been conducted with the Navajo nation of Arizona and New Mexico. Until the middle of the 20th century, Western medical care was only minimally available. Those facilities that did exist were understaffed or employed underqualified workers. Thus, the Navajo were understandably reluctant to seek such care. In the last 40 years, however, increased funding and staffing of clinics and hospitals on Native American reservations have improved the availability and quality of care, and many Navajo are now more willing to seek nontraditional care. Most notably, prenatal and postnatal care for expectant mothers and their newborns has improved enough that infant and maternal mortality rates have declined, and childbirth in a hospital has become safer than it was previously for both infant and mother.

Changes in Navajo family structure and work patterns have also affected the ways in which they avail themselves of hospital services. The Navajo traditionally have lived in large, extended-family households, making their livings as farmers and herders. When people got sick, they were easily cared for by family members. Today, however, many Navajo live in smaller family units and earn their livings outside the home, so family members are often unable to care for their sick or elderly relatives. Consequently, they tend to rely on hospitals more frequently and for more health problems than in the past. Only in remote areas of the Navajo

A Native American brush church, complete with cross and bells, stands as an example of the continued relationship between Native American rituals and Christian practices.

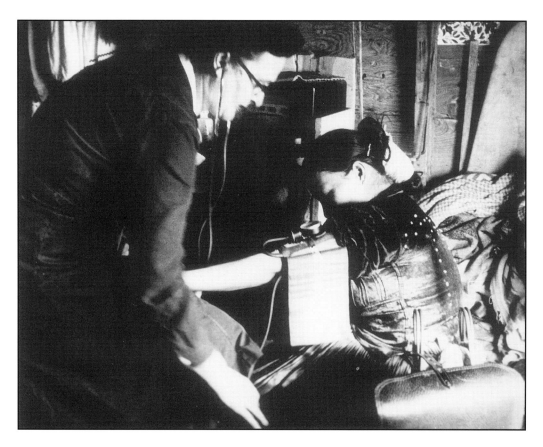

A United States Public Health Service worker monitors the blood pressure of a Native American woman. As hospital conditions on reservations have improved and survival rates have risen, the percentage of Native Americans who seek Western medical care has risen dramatically.

nation, where hospitals and clinics are lacking, are traditional healing methods still predominant.

In the 1950s, the federal government and the government of the Navajo nation began working together to train and certify Navajos as medical para-professionals in a variety of health-care delivery programs. At the time, the majority of Navajo health workers spoke only their native language, so some were also trained as interpreters. Others became community health workers, providing information to the Navajo about United States Public Health Service programs and facilities.

The Navajo and United States governments also cosponsored programs through which traditional healers learned about Western medical procedures and Western physicians and health administrators learned the importance of adapting their techniques to Navajo beliefs and customs. Navajo curatives and rituals that succeeded in treating ailments with psychological or emotional components were also scrutinized by medical doctors. In the 1960s, recognizing the possible advantages of traditional healing ceremonies, the United States Public Health Service on the Navajo nation initiated a policy whereby some patients were referred to healers for treatment.

The importance of cooperation between Western and Native American medical practitioners is sharply illustrated by a 1953 incident at a facility for tuberculosis patients in Tucson, Arizona. One day, Navajo patients suddenly left the facility en masse. Annie Wauneka, the head of the Navajo Health Committee, asked why they had left. The patients replied that they would not stay in the building because a tree on the hospital grounds had been struck by lightning. Knowing that Navajos believe that lightning is a dangerous, disease-causing natural force, Wauneka arranged for a traditional healer to perform a

"Blessingway" ceremony to purify the hospital. Once the rite was completed and the dangerous contamination from lightning had been eliminated, the patients returned.

Many of the findings from the Navajo nation studies are applicable to Native American communities throughout North America. Although conventional medicine is deemed useful for serious, complex, or life-threatening conditions, traditional treatments offer reassurance, emotional support, and the restoration of physical and spiritual harmony that has always been at the core of traditional Native American medical practices.

Today, Native American healing techniques are often maintained as a reflection of tribal and personal identity. Healing rituals not only administer to the physical body; they also restore one's emotional and spiritual well-being. Believers continue to rely on traditional remedies and to perform and participate in healing rituals not only for their medical efficacy but also for the spiritual vitality that they impart.

BIBLIOGRAPHY

Basso, Keith. *The Cibecue Apache*. New York: Holt, Rinehart & Winston, 1970.

Boaz, Franz. *Kwakiutl Ethnography*. Chicago: University of Chicago Press, 1966.

Eastman, Charles. *The Soul of the Indian: An Interpretation*. Lincoln: University of Nebraska Press, 1980.

Fenton, William. "Contacts Between Iroquois, Herbalism and Colonial Medicine." In *Smithsonian Report for 1941*. Washington, D.C.: Smithsonian Institution, 1942.

Fogelson, Raymond. "Change, Persistence, and Accommodation in Cherokee Medico-Magical Beliefs." In *Symposium on Cherokee and Iroquois Culture*. Washington, D.C.: Smithsonian Institution, 1961.

Gill, Sam. *Native American Religions*. Belmont, CA: Wadsworth Publishing, 1982.

Gilmore, Melvin. *Uses Of Plants by the Indians of the Missouri River Region*. Lincoln: University of Nebraska Press, 1991.

Hariot, Thomas. *A Brief and True Report of the New Found Land of Virginia*. 1590. Reprint, New York: Dover Books, 1972.

Jones, David. *Sanapia: Comanche Medicine Woman*. Prospect Heights, IL: Waveland Press, 1984.

Kunitz, Stephen. *Disease Change and the Role of Medicine: The Navajo Experience*. Berkeley: University of California Press, 1983.

Lafitau, J. F. *Customs of the American Indians*. Paris: n.p., 1724.

Lange, Charles. *Cochiti: A New Mexico Pueblo, Past and Present*. Carbondale: Southern Illinois University Press, 1959.

Neihardt, John, ed. *Black Elk Speaks*. Lincoln: University of Nebraska Press, 1961.

Ortiz, Alfonso, ed. *Handbook of North American Indians*. Washington, D.C.: Smithsonian Institution, 1983.

Radin, Paul. *The Autobiography of a Winnebago Indian*. New York: Dover Publications, 1963.

Sagard, Gabriel. *The Long Journey to the Country of the Hurons*. Toronto: Champlains Society, 1939.

Tedlock, Dennis, and Barbara Tedlock, eds. *Teachings from the American Earth*. New York: Liveright, 1975.

Thornton, Russell. *American Indian Holocaust and Survival: A Population History Since 1492*. Norman: University of Oklahoma Press, 1987.

Thwaites, R. G., ed. *Jesuit Relations and Allied Documents, 1610-1791*. Cleveland: Burrows Brothers, n.d.

U.S. Department of Commerce, Bureau of the Census. *American Indian and Alaska Native Areas 1990*. CP-1-1A. Washington, D.C.: U.S. Department of Commerce, Bureau of the Census, 1990.

Vogel, Virgil. *American Indian Medicine*. Norman: University of Oklahoma Press, 1970.

Walker, D., Jr., ed. *Witchcraft and Sorcery of the American Native Peoples*. Moscow, ID: University of Idaho Press, 1989.

GLOSSARY

aboriginal The first to be present in a region; a native.

angakot A type of Inuit healer who helps retrieve people's souls when they have become separated from their bodies.

assimilation Adoption by individuals of the practices of another, usually dominant, society; a means by which the host society recruits new members and replaces a subordinate society's culture. The United States, as well as most Native American societies, gained new members in this manner.

astringent A substance that draws together the soft tissues of the body, thereby restricting bleeding or preventing harmful substances from entering.

cathartic A healing agent that clears the bowel and eliminates harmful substances from the body.

chantway A long and elaborate Navajo healing ritual, also known as a sing, during which supernatural powers are called upon to remove from a patient's body the harmful effects of contaminating agents.

medicine society A tribal organization of Native American healers whose members specialize in treatments and ritual cures for particular ailments.

diuretic A substance that increases the flow of urine from the body, thereby reducing swelling.

efficacy The power to produce an effect; effectiveness.

hallucinogen A substance that induces intense visions by acting upon the human nervous system.

healer A Native American who has been trained to cure illnesses by using natural substances and performing rituals that eliminate the underlying causes of disorders.

medicine bag A pouch made of soft animal hide or cloth used by Native American healers to carry natural remedies, non-botanical medicines, and instruments for extracting foreign objects.

patent medicine A packaged nonprescription drug that is protected by a trademark but whose contents are not completely disclosed. Patent medicines became popular in the late 18th century and often capitalized on the effectiveness of traditional Native American treatments.

peyote A small spineless cactus that grows in northern Mexico and southern Texas and that causes hallucinations when ingested by humans. Peyote is considered a sacred plant by some Native Americans who consume it in special religious rituals.

Peyotist A person who believes that peyote has special spiritual powers and ingests it for religious purposes.

pharmacopoeia A collection or stock of drugs and curative substances, especially one issued by an officially recognized authority and serving as a standard.

poultice A soft and usually heated mixture of curative substances applied to sores or other skin ailments.

sweat lodge A specially designed structure, made of animal skin stretched over a wooden frame, which is heated and filled with steam. Sweat therapy is used by Native Americans for curative and religious purposes.

taboo A ritual restriction on a person's behavior intended to protect from supernatural harm.

INDEX

PICTURE CREDITS

NANCY BONVILLAIN has a Ph.D. in anthropology from Columbia University. Dr. Bonvillain has written a grammar book and dictionary of the Mohawk language as well as 12 Chelsea House titles, including *The Mohawk* (1992), *Black Hawk* (1994), *The Teton Sioux* (1994), *The Zuni* (1995), and *Native American Religion* (1996). She has also written two textbooks, *Language, Culture, and Communication* and *Women and Men: Cultural Constructs of Gender*.

FRANK W. PORTER III, general editor of INDIANS OF NORTH AMERICA, is director of the Chelsea House Foundation for American Indian Studies. He holds a B.A., M.A., and Ph.D. from the University of Maryland. He has done extensive research concerning the Indians of Maryland and Delaware and is the author of numerous articles on their history, archaeology, geography, and ethnography. He was formerly director of the Maryland Commission on Indian Affairs and American Indian Research and Resource Institute, Gettysburg, Pennsylvania, and he has received grants from the Delaware Humanities Forum, the Maryland Committee for the Humanities, the Ford Foundation, and the National Endowment for the Humanities, among others. Dr. Porter is the author of *The Bureau of Indian Affairs* in the Chelsea House KNOW YOUR GOVERNMENT series.